Teach Internal Locus of Control

A Positive Psychology App

Teach Internal Locus of Control

Russ Hill

Teach Internal Locus of Control: A Positive Psychology App
2nd Printing, 2013
Copyright © 2011 by Russ Hill
ISBN 978-0-9833464-0-1
WILL TO POWER PRESS, Beach Haven, NJ

For more information please contact: www.teachinternalcontrol.com.
Psychology/Achievement/Self-help/Academics/Internal Control

Editing and book design by Harvard Girl Word Services
www.harvardgirledits.com
Original cover artwork by Joanne Levine;
recreated for use here by Harvard Girl Word Services

For "George"

Note from author: You will see that I have chosen to use the masculine pronoun "he" in many cases throughout this book, with some feminine pronouns from time to time. My decision is not gender-biased, but simply an effort to make the material as easy to read and understand as possible.

Acknowledgments

I wish to gratefully acknowledge the help and support of the following individuals and institutions: Lyndon Baines Johnson, the "Education President," and the National Institute of Education; Research For Better Schools, Inc., along with Anita Simon and Gil Boyer, my immediate supervisors, and the many staff members who worked with me; my editor Heidi Connolly; my research assistant Rita Halpert; and Craig Henry who inspired me to finally write this book by musing on the question, "What makes the difference?"

Table of Contents

Introduction

I have two grandsons. One is a self-directed jet and the other is a ship without a captain. What makes the difference?

Both these young men are about the same age, one 23 and the other 25. Both have had excellent social and educational opportunities. Both are physically well, and both are very intelligent. Yet there is a stark contrast in their level of achievement and happiness to date. Why?

"Eric" (not his real name), the older of the two and the self-directed jet, completed his undergraduate college work with a B++ average, majoring in a challenging philosophy program and picking up the equivalent of majors in both journalism and business at the same time. In the extracurricular world, he has become qualified as a wilderness instructor and a rock-climbing instructor, working in a ski shop and experiencing the joy and exhilaration that comes with achieving a high level of skiing performance. Eric had a great time in college, and continued to take courses in the summer after his formal graduation in order to complete the business curriculum. In fact, he was so enthusiastic that eventually the university had to tell him enough was enough to get him to stop taking classes. Now, after working three years at a prestigious international personnel firm, Eric is making an amazing amount of money, flying around the Pacific Rim, working on interesting projects, and is on track to become a partner in his company. Fantastic!

"George," on the other hand, the younger, "undirected ship," started out in college majoring in mathematics. Although he qualified for advanced placement he dropped out in his second semester. He was living at home and faked going to class. He said the college counselor had given him poor guidance. His next attempt was at an excellent local community college where the same thing happened. This time he said his courses were boring. For a time George worked at a restaurant at night for tips and a low hourly wage. He usually went out with friends and acquaintances after work and slept late in the morning, regularly indulging in marijuana use. This became his pattern of choice. At some point he started a tech program at the community college, but again cut his classes and dropped out. School "wasn't interesting," it seemed, was "too much drudgery." Recently, George was out with his server acquaintances late after work and driving drunk. When he smashed his car into a tree he and the others were badly hurt. Currently, he is hanging out at his father's home, convalescing, working as a server part time while waiting for his case to be heard before a judge. Where is George going? Nowhere—except possibly to jail. Upsetting! Disappointing!

What is the difference between these two young men? I maintain that Eric, the self-directed jet, believes that the direction, or *location of control*, of his life lies within his influence. He is an "achiever," an agent, an "origin," who sets goals and works effectively to attain them. He is focused, and believes that he is responsible for the course his life will take.

George, however, believes that the location of control of his life lies *outside* his influence. He is a "re-actor" who allows himself to be pushed around by his immediate moods and feelings and by the expectations and demands of others. George is unfocused, and believes he is not the one responsible for the course of his life; that others and other forces are.

The differences between Eric and George become obvious when you talk to them. Eric is vital and enthusiastic. He recently told his mother that he would be tied up for the following two weeks because he was expecting to have to put in 80 hours per week to be able to complete several important projects. This was not onerous to him. In fact, it was challenging and exciting. George, on the other hand, is lethargic and uncommunicative. His life is more about waiting… hanging out. He tends to act on passing impulses, and has no plans and no goals. His day's activities are dictated by waves of emotional shifts, and by trying to please and impress his current friends in trivial and insignificant ways. In essence, Eric believes he can internally influence the course of his life, where George believes that his life is largely influenced by external forces.

. . .

This book is dedicated to George. You see, I love both of my grandsons. There is no need to worry about Eric. He is happy and challenged, and I need only stand back and observe with wonder and pleasure his approach to life. But I am deeply concerned about George who is not happy and who is in a downward spiral. He is the biblical prodigal son. I often think about him and worry about him, though I have no influence with him. Perhaps if George were to read this book he might understand that there are other possibilities. Perhaps he might consider asserting more internal control over his life. Perhaps he would begin to see that his efforts can result in achievement and happiness. Were I to see such a transformation begin to happen, I would be there to welcome him with a coat, metaphorically speaking, of many colors.

In this book we call individuals like Eric, who believe they can influence the course of their own lives, "Internals." We call individuals like George, who believe they have little or no influence over the course of their lives, "Externals."

Figure 1: The Locus of Control model.

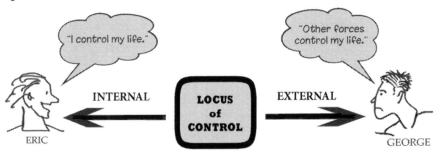

Let's step back for a moment. If you are a parent, think of your children; if you are a teacher, think of your pupils; if you are a supervisor, think of your workers. Can you place the individuals in your group somewhere on this Internal-External continuum? Internals have a sense of direction and feel responsible for getting things done. They are self-starters. They schedule and anticipate tasks, and they feel responsible for the success or failure of their own efforts. Externals tend to be lackadaisical, seek to avoid responsibility, wait to be told what to do, and do not believe that their own success or failure is their responsibility.

Are these distinctions between Internals and Externals important? Would you like to be able to teach others to be Internals? If so, read on because this book will:

- Provide a deeper understanding of the concept of internal location of control;
- Present overwhelming evidence of the importance of internal control for individual happiness, achievement, and worldly success;

- Show you how to teach internal control to others and thereby increase their effectiveness and happiness;
- Provide research evidence validating the effectiveness of the instructional procedures outlined;
- Suggest curriculum designs and effective tools for teaching internal control, including concepts, skills, and learner activities; and
- Suggest how internal control can be taught and employed in families, schools, colleges, and workplaces to improve personal effectiveness, learning, and feelings of well-being.

In effect, once you have read this book, whether you are a teacher, parent, supervisor, or health-care worker, you will immediately be able to teach internal control to others for their—and your—overall life enhancement and success.

Stunning and significant results

These instructional ideas and procedures have been validated in a large-scale evaluation study and have been found to be successful in teaching children to become more internal in *both* belief and behavior (see Chapter 4 for details). *Let me say that again: this instructional strategy has been proven successful.* That means that we can...you can...*anyone* can teach internal control by integrating this content and employing these techniques.

These ideas are not based on speculation! These ideas and procedures have been experimentally tested and validated where it counts—with real people in real situations.

Finally, there is a personal dividend for you if you explore these ideas. Read this book and *you* will become more "internal." You will improve your competence to achieve your goals and enhance your sense of personal well-being and happiness. Doesn't that inspire you to turn to Chapter 1...*now?*

Chapter 1

What Is Internal Locus of Control?

Locus of control is what we in the behavioral sciences call a psychological construct; that is, an idea about human behavior that has been created to describe a group of attitudes and behaviors. Believing in the idea that there is a *locus,* or "location," of control, and that people's lives are affected by this belief, has been studied by many people for many years. Not only has it been discussed, argued, and criticized as a concept, but a very large number of articles in academic journals and at least one book have been devoted to the topic (see *Locus of Control: Current trends in Theory and Research* by H. Lefcourt).[1] For example, the 1966 Monograph introducing the construct was the third most cited publication between 1965 and 1975 in the Social Science Citation Index[2] *(http://mres.gmu.edu/readings/PSYC557/Rotter1990.pdf)*. With that said, we can probably all agree that locus of control is not a concept that is familiar to the general public. I would venture to say that this is mostly due to the fact that there is little understanding of its meaning, and therefore very little awareness of its significance.

Contrast this unfamiliarity with the general public's awareness of other psychological concepts like self-esteem and fear of failure, ideas which have long been incorporated into our culture's language and lexicon. It is my hope that this book (and future ones like it) will increase the lagging public awareness about this particular construct precisely because it is so effective for dealing with the important issues of daily life.

Before we discuss locus of control in detail, let's look at how we can tell where an individual might place on a scale that measures how much or how little they believe that they have the ability to influence the course of their lives.

Attitude Surveys

One way we can measure whether someone approaches life from an internal or external perspective, as described in the Introduction to this book, is to have them rate themselves on the Rotter Internal-External (I-E) Scale.[3] The Rotter Scale has become the most widely recognized instrument constructed to measure an individual's locus of control attitude; that is, whether the individual believes he has or does not have influence over the course of his life. The Rotter Scale, developed by Jules Rotter and his associates in 1962 and building on the work of others, uses a numerical scale based on the results of a questionnaire to measure an individual's belief about how he expects his life to unfold.[4-5] This questionnaire presents pairs of statements and asks the subject to select the statement in each pair with which he or she most strongly agrees. For example, in the two pairs of statements below taken from Rotter's questionnaire, would you choose (a) or (b)?

a. Becoming a success is a matter of hard work; luck has little or nothing to do with it.
b. Getting a good job depends mainly on being in the right place at the right time.

a.   In the long run, people get the respect they deserve in this world.

b.   Unfortunately, an individual's worth often passes unrecognized, no matter how hard he tries.

Rotter's survey is often used to provide baseline descriptions of subject populations in numerous psychological and sociological studies. Various researchers have adapted this original scale to create customized measures to study selected groups according to age, culture, vocation, physical or mental health, alcohol-related behavior, and so on.[6-21] (You may access and download a description and review of 28 Measures of Locus of Control at *teachinternalcontrol. com/uploads/LOC_Measures_1.pdf*.) If you use these measures, however, you should be aware of a minor issue of reliability because a subject's belief can be influenced by his understanding of the aim of the measurement. For example, if you were to take one of these surveys right now, your score would not be as valid as it might have been before you started reading this book because now you know something about the basic concept. That is, you know what locus of behavior *is* and you know about the nature of Internals and Externals. With a sense of the basic concept it would not be at all difficult for you to guess which response would be that of an Internal and which of an External, and you might be motivated to respond in a way you consider more "correct" or perhaps more socially desirable.

A Continuum of Belief

As we talked about earlier, locus of control can be viewed as a continuum, where one pole is the belief that you can influence the course of your life and the other pole is the belief that you cannot influence the course of your life. In filling out a questionnaire like Rotter's, we are placing ourselves at some point on this continuum. Those of us who place nearer the pole representing a positive belief in our ability to influence our destinies are called Internals because we are demonstrating internality. Those of us who score on the continuum nearer the pole representing a lack of belief in our power to influence our lives are called Externals because we are demonstrating externality. In the real world, of course, individuals are neither "pure" Internals nor Externals.

Locus of control is just another way to say...

Understanding that we all have a belief about our location of control and that we only vary in our relative placement on the measurement scale takes us a step further toward understanding the concept behind the words. One way to increase our comprehension is to relate this term to other popular terms and buzz words in our culture, terms that we know because they are used in our speech, media, and schools. For example, take the term *self-directed*. We all know that self-directed people believe that they can control, or at least strongly influence, the direction of their lives. Therefore, in terms of a locus of control, we can say that these individuals are clearly Internal or that they behave with internality.

Now consider the term *empowered*. Those who are empowered, or act and feel as if they are empowered, are also Internals. Empowered individuals generally are not victims. They believe and act as if they have the power to steer the ship that is their life.

How about the term *responsible*? If people believe they have the option to be accountable and act responsibly, then they believe they have the power to decide what to do and how to live as they travel the course of their lives. Surely, these individuals could be labeled Internals as well. And the same is true for those we would describe as having an *independent* bent. Valuing independence and believing in one's ability to be independent and live independently would also put one on the internal side of our scale.

Did you notice that all these qualities are considered desirable and worthy of pursuit in today's culture?

What internal control is not

With all these definitions, you might be wondering if there is any difference at all between having self-control and having an internal locus of control. The answer to this question is definitely yes. The difference lies in the fact that self-control is limited to personal restraint in that it is the ability to constrain one's behavior or emotions in a difficult situation. As such, it involves the act of *not* doing something. Internal control, on the other hand, is much more. Although internal control encompasses the element of self-control, it is also concerned with the directing of and managing of one's life. Internals may practice self-control, but not as a response to external influences like religious doctrine or social pressure. Instead, they use their ability to exercise self-control for reasons of their own.

If self-control is not the same as internal control, what about *self-esteem*? Most of us are familiar with the concept of self-esteem, typically defined as the confidence in one's own worth and abilities. Doesn't self-esteem sound a lot like internal control? Aren't both of them desirable and predictors of success, effectiveness, and happiness?

In reality, research shows that although having self-esteem and having a high level of internal control often correlate, they are actually independent of one another.[22] I'll explain. We know, for example, that Internals tend to have a high level of self-esteem, and we know that Internals usually feel confident, at least part or a lot of the time. But sometimes Internals experience failure and depression related to their failures. It is at these times, when Internals tend to doubt their abilities and lack confidence, that an inverse relationship between internal control and self-esteem can be found to exist. The bottom line is that Internals in these situations often feel terrible about themselves. Externals, however, squarely placed on the other side of the continuum, may continue to feel "good" about themselves regardless of whether they experience a perceived failure.[23]

Another important difference between internal control and self-esteem is that internal control correlates positively with achievement,[24-29] whereas self-esteem does not always do so.[30] Why? It may be that those who have high self-esteem are not being realistic about their situation…the adolescent boy who thinks he is doing well in school when he is actually failing, for instance. Interestingly, in the field of psychology, the validity of self-esteem as a predictor of any behavior is in question for reasons like this.[31-35]

Another thing internal control *is not* is the belief in unlimited achievement. Over time, our culture has propagated the belief, one espoused by many teachers and motivational speakers, that "you can be anything you want to be." These inspirational leaders would have us believe that there are no limits on what we can become and what we can achieve, except due to the limits of our own imagination, conception, and will. And although there may be value in looking at the world this way, this is not what we mean by "internality." Since true Internals are sensitive to the limits of reality and are clear about these limits, they do not conceive themselves to be all-powerful. For example, an Internal who is unable to walk or is otherwise physically challenged will recognize the situation for what it is—a currently real limitation—and will accepted the limitation as such.

Yet, while it is true that Internals tend to accept the limitations of circumstances they cannot change, they also continue to seek to influence those factors in their life over which they *can* exercise some control. Sensitive to the areas of their lives that can be influenced and shaped, they work to effect change in those areas. In this manner, they fully accept and practice the ideas embedded in the first stanza of the *Serenity Prayer* by Reinhold Niebuhr: "God grant me the serenity/to accept the things I cannot change/courage to change the things I can/ and wisdom to know the difference." This is opposed to Externals, who surrender to the limitations of their situation, holding that such situations don't allow them (or people like them) to have a real chance in life.

More about being internal

Since it is not the purpose of this book to provide a review of all the work related to the broad topic of the locus of control, and since it *is* our goal to explore the question of how internal control can be taught and applied, I will keep the next section brief. For those interested, a much wider and growing body of research on the subject of locus of control can easily be perused on the Internet. To that end, one of the most historically important books on the subject is the one mentioned earlier by Herbert Lefcourt. This book provides a professional in-depth discussion of the findings, issues, and nuances of this psychological construct.[36]

Internal Control: General or Domain-specific?

Most theorists think of internal control as a general characteristic: that is, that a person can have a general internal or general external attitude toward all of life's activities. This is probably true to some degree, but it is a question that is still under discussion and debate in the world of psychology. In my own experience, I find that it is useful to think of internal control as something that is more *domain-specific*, where one may be an Internal in one or many of the sectors, or "domains," of life, but not necessarily in all of them.

For example, you may be an excellent teacher. In this case, your internal control score would lean toward the internal side of the scale if the internal control inventory questions focused on teaching and educationally related activities. However, let's say that although you know a lot about teaching, you don't know a thing about auto mechanics. In fact, you're the kind of person who feels fairly inadequate in that area…so inadequate that when you have car trouble you throw up your hands and refuse to even enter the work area of an automotive shop. Why? Because in your way of thinking, the mechanical problem is something that just happened. It's not your fault. After all, how could you be expected to know that you were supposed to have done X, Y, or Z to maintain the engine? If this way of thinking sounds familiar, it may be because you are exhibiting the traits of an External, at least in the domain of automotive repair.

Again, the difference lies in one's perspective. Individuals with a generalized belief in internal control believe that if they decide to expend the time and energy to do it, they can become proficient in almost any new domain. Using our example, although you are a teacher (and a good one), and expect to keep your energy focused on your selected domain of teaching, you might also believe that you can learn to become a competent auto mechanic if you should choose apply yourself in that way.

This difference in internality in different domains is relevant to teaching learners in two ways. First, when teaching internal control, the learning needs to take place within the context of a specific domain, such as auto mechanics. Second, learners need to be guided in learning to transfer their internal attitudes in one domain to other domains…and to a general posture toward the world.

Opportunity influences direction

Psychologists have found that internality is associated with opportunity.[37] This means that wealthy individuals who are generally presented with more opportunities are more often internal in their approach to life. The other side of this equation is that individuals who live in poverty and have fewer opportunities tend to approach life with more of the External's perspective.

Several studies support the contention that there are three different factors related to opportunity that influence internality: class, race, and family stability. For instance, children of a lower socioeconomic class are generally found to be more external,[38-40] and seldom rise to the level of internality representative of middle- or upper-class children.

On average, African American children and African American adults score more externally than their white counterparts[41-5] and being black *and* of a lower socioeconomic strata further increases the probability of an external score. Living in an unstable family environment also predicts an external score.[46-8] But in all these cases, investigators hypothesize that the children who are "lower class," black, or from unstable families score more externally because of their lack of opportunity.

There are two important concepts that we can take away from these studies. First, identifying specific groups of individuals who need and can benefit from the teaching of internal control (lower socioeconomic level children, black children, and children from unstable families) is a significant step in providing equality of educational opportunity for all. Second, once we identify the groups in need, we should create support and opportunities for these learners.

Can Internality Be Taught?

The short answer to the question, "Can internality be taught?" is "Yes, definitely," and evidence of this fact can be found in the intervention program literature describing treatments that are, in fact, reported to be effective. These treatments are: (1) the creation of special environments that emphasize and reward internal behavior through their structure and activities;[49-50] (2) counseling and therapy approaches in which clients are guided in the process of examining and identifying the internal-external qualities of their personal behaviors;[51] and (3) direct school training in attitudes and behaviors believed to be directly related to internal control.[52-3]

Let's start with the first treatment, *special environmental influences*. When Nowicki and Barnes (1973) studied inner city teenagers, they reported that the teenagers gained in internal control by participating in a one-week structured camp program that emphasized working together to accomplish goals. This gain in internality continued to increase for those children who later returned for an additional week of camping. The authors suggest that emphasizing self-responsibility to the youngsters during their camping experience made them feel more in control of events and better able to see the connection between their behavior and its effects, thus enabling them to feel reinforced for their growth in internality.

Lifshitz (1973) also suggested that environment plays a role in determining locus of control. In this case, researchers found a significant difference in internality between children who lived in two different *kibbutzim*, where the children with higher internal scores came from the *kibbutz* in which they were allowed considerable autonomy from an early age, while the children with lower internal scores came from the *kibbutz* in which patriarchal authority and dominance was the accepted practice. This author concluded that an environment that encourages decision making, self-dependence, and individual action is also one that fosters internality.

Counseling and therapy is the second kind of treatment that offers an opportunity for learning—that is, increasing—locus of control. This approach looks at attitudes that influence individuals to behave internally, and provides data that supports the contention that internality can be taught directly. Reimanis (1970), for example, established a three-month program of weekly counseling sessions for a small group of first and third graders.[54] When these children, identified as "behavior-problem" children, met individually for counseling sessions with their teachers, the teachers identified what seemed to be reinforcing to each child and then used it to point out behavior-effect contingencies. It is interesting to note that not only did the children participating in the program show significantly increased internality over the children in the control group, but anecdotal reports also reflected an increase in behaviors associated with internal control—that is, self-direction, interest level, participation in projects, and self-responsibility.

Reimanis used similar techniques with college students. In this program, the students participated in 45-minute group counseling sessions held once a week for 10 weeks. During these sessions, counselors encouraged the students to discuss their personal problems, to replace external responses with internal responses, and to consider how to use internal responses to plan for future events. Again, the experimental group showed a significant increase in internality over their counterparts in the control group. More specifically, narrative records indicated that the students began talking about taking more personal responsibility and began to behave with more internality in their daily lives. For example, the students could now be seen to be making decisions about new living quarters, changing academic programs, and seeking out instructors to discuss their academic status. (Other studies have approximately replicated these effects as well.[55])

Our third intervention approach is a direct method for *teaching attitudes and behaviors that are believed to foster internality*. In this case, DeCharms, et al (1972) sought to foster "personal causation" or "origin" behavior in both teachers and students through a program for inner-city African American youngsters in a Midwestern elementary school. DeCharms specified that to help individuals be "origins" (to be internally motivated, where behavior originates from within) they must be guided to: determine realistic goals for themselves; know their own strengths and weaknesses; determine concrete actions that will help them reach their goals; and learn to evaluate the progress they are making toward their objectives. In this case, DeCharms reported that when teachers treated their students as origins, the children began to exhibit more "origin-like" behaviors than the students who did not participate in the program. Furthermore, evidence revealed that fostering personal causation also played a role in improving students' academic achievement scores. (Note: DeCharms' work has been a major influence upon the creation of the instructional program described later in this book.)

Achievement and Internality

One of the more interesting facets of internal control is its strong connection to achievement. As you will see in the next chapter, many studies report that a positive belief in internal control correlates with the sense of achievement and accomplishment in many domains. In other words, those who are significant achievers are also predictably Internal, and those who are Internal predictably achieve.

Hmm…so here we are confronted with the classic logical puzzle that such a "correlation" always presents:

1. Does positive internal control cause successful achievement?
2. Does having the experience of successful achievement cause more positive internal control scores?
3. Is there a third factor in operation here that somehow affects both achievement and internality?
4. Is there some kind of interaction between internal control and achievement? or…
5. Is this simply a wildly unusual repeating coincidence?

Let's start with the last possibility first (#5). I believe that we can immediately eliminate the hypotheses that this is a repeating coincidence simply because it occurs way, *way* too often.

Now let's consider possibility #3, whether there might be a third factor causing achievement and internality. I believe that hypothetically there may well be. One example is Rotter's consideration of the idea that his scale might be measuring "achievement motivation,"[19] where achievement motivation could be considered to cause both achievement and internality. In this case, however, we actually tried to influence achievement motivation in our instructional program (the one presented in this book), but were unable to find any measurable effect. So, in essence, though I will admit that achievement motivation may theoretically be an underlying factor of both achievement and internal control, there is no way I have personally found to validate or utilize this hypothesis.

Others researchers have hypothesized that achievement in and of itself causes a more positive belief in internal control based on the fact that successful achievement spawns belief in internal control and failure is habitually a source of belief in external control (possibility #2). A recent study by Hong[56] and his associates, for example, makes this case based on a study of 1,150 students where the researchers concluded that higher academic achievement both preceded and led students to a higher level of belief in internal control.

Teacher lore supports this view, as evidenced by feedback from Janet Hartman, an elementary school teacher and personal friend, and a woman recognized for her success in teaching severely economically and educationally disadvantaged children in the city of Philadelphia. When I asked Janet for the key to her success she said that she had to find the one thing at which each new class could succeed, because once the students experienced their first successful achievement they became more confident and could begin to work successfully on the rest of the curriculum. It was feeling that first critical success that made it possible for each new class to keep going. I have shared this account with several other teachers, who agree with Janet's assessment and tell me that in their work with individual children their aim is to have the child experience just one success, after which the child is more likely to begin to progress onward.

But wait! Conversely, there are many studies that can be interpreted to support the hypothesis that higher internality *predicts* achievement...and therefore can be hypothesized to *influence* achievement (possibility #1). Again and again measures of internal control successfully predict who will achieve more and who will not. In these cases, positive internal control clearly precedes achievement (a necessary condition of cause). So which is it? Does a positive belief in internal control dispose successful achievement...or does the experience of achievement dispose a more internal score?

Perhaps it is both. Perhaps the relationship between achievement and internal control is more of a closed system, a kind of circular interaction (possibility #4).

Let's say you're just learning to play golf. At your first lesson you are pleased because you experience some moderate success. Based on this success you expect to progress at your next lesson, too, although you still may be timid or hesitant in your approach. However, when your swing improves as expected and desired you recognize the fact that you are indeed making progress. By the next lesson you are no longer hesitant; instead you come determined to succeed. Now that you have gained a sense of control, you also sense that if you apply yourself you will most certainly improve your golf game. Because you are enjoying this successful endeavor, you believe *you can keep doing it*. You can do it! You can achieve in golf!

This attitude of success and eagerness to keep improving disposes you to keep achieving, and it is this ongoing process that becomes a circular interaction of:

Achievement > Positive Internal Control >
Achievement > Positive Internal Control >

…and so on. I like to describe this interaction as spiral in nature. In this case, where positive achievement correlates to an increasing sense of internal control, we can say you are experiencing an upward or positive spiral (see Figure 2).

Figure 2: The Achievement > Internal Control upward spiral.

Increased Belief in
Internal Control

Increased Belief in
Internal Control

Achievement

Achievement

Several researchers share the hypothesis that there is an interactive relationship between achievement and internality. Two examples come to mind, including that of the Hong research group mentioned above. These authors end their paper with the following statement, "Experiencing higher academic achievement should support a belief in competence and a higher sense of perceived control, which in turn would result in subsequent higher achievement." Hmm…Does this not sound like the upward spiral?

The other example involves the work of the iconic James S. Coleman and his team of researchers of the landmark "Coleman Report"[57] that analyzed the records of 150,000 students and found that "[The relationship between achievement and internality] may very well be two-directional with both the attitude and the achievement affecting each other."

It is important to recognize that these two teams of researchers are not simply psychological theoreticians who are advocates of internal locus of control, but specialists, authorities in the analysis of large data bases. They have no axe to grind. They are professionals who reached their conclusions based on their work with massive amounts of real world data that comes from measuring academic achievement and related variables, such as school organization, teacher preparation, patterns of student home life, peer culture, economic levels, and race.

Given the extensiveness of these knowledge bases and the agreement of these eminent researchers and others, we feel confident in basing our methodology for teaching internal control on the assumption that achievement and belief in internal control are interactive correlates.

From Here Forward

Now, in the context of our discussion of achievement and internality I would like to restate the objective of this book: to enable you to teach internal control and empower those you teach to move in a continuous upward spiral of **achievement> belief in internal control > achievement >**.

But before we proceed to learn how to teach internality, I want to further address the reasons for teaching internal control, as presented in the next chapter. I believe you will find the theory and data that supports the desirability of teaching internal locus of control to be both amazing and inspiring.

Chapter 2

Why Teach Internal Locus of Control?

If I could teach my children, my students, or my employees one thing, it would be internality. Why? Because internality is power. It is freedom. It is excitement! It leads to academic success, to self-improvement, to better health, to worldly success, to significant accomplishment, to happiness, and more.

In popular terms, we want those we love to be self-directed rather than directed by others. We want those for whom we care to take responsibility for their actions rather than to attribute the reason for their behavior to others. We want them to be empowered, rather than feel like victims and believe that the power belongs to others. We want them to be thoughtful purposeful agents who act effectively and are successful out in the world.

In philosophical terms, believing in internal control encapsulates the highest ideal of personhood. Internality is the quintessence of being human and of being a member of the human species: to be a thinking, conscious "actor," one who takes responsibility for his own behavior, sets his own goals, and works effectively to obtain them.

This is the definition of the highest level of human behavior—of the conscious agent moving effectively in the world. This is also more than Plato's ideal of the "examined life," for it is inclusive of Plato's ideal and moves beyond it.

There are other possibilities, of course. You might wish to teach group cohesiveness...or obedience...or even helplessness, subservience, dependence, or compliance. We know that these qualities can be taught and are being taught every day by parents, teachers, leaders, and dictators. So, let me say here that if you wish to teach any of these qualities as a primary objective, teaching the methods of internal control is definitely not for you.

That is not to say that those who are internal will not be obedient or compliant, but that primarily they will be independent. And that once they feel established as independent individuals, they will feel free to choose to be compliant and obedient or not. The key term here is *choice*. For example, an Internal may choose to submit to the discipline of a religious order or may be willing to submit to the discipline of a harsh coach or the demands of a strict music teacher. But in each case, the individual will *make his own decision*.

It is tempting for me to take the time to offer arguments that relate a belief in internal control to some well-known philosophical positions. I find a similarity between much of Nietzsche's concept of "will to power" and internality, for example, because I interpret Nietzsche's concept of power to mean, in the main, power over oneself. And is not internality a psychological description of Sartre's "existential man," of Dewey's ideal "pragmatic person," or of Maslow's "self-actualizing" person?

But it is not my purpose, nor do I want to invest the space here in this context, to relate these philosophical positions in detail. Ideas like these are fun to examine and discuss, but I suggest that the best way to explore these questions is to do so in the evening with a gimlet in hand (vodka, please), and on those pleasant occasions remind myself to sip slowly or risk losing focus and letting the conversation wander to other topics.

It is also not my purpose in this book to suggest relationships between internality and some of the great philosophical positions of our culture in order to justify the desirability of teaching internality. In fact, I mention these connections only to suggest that internality might be considered a measurable quality that is the very epitome of human uniqueness. In an ideal world, everyone would be internal. Am I overreaching? Perhaps, but think about it as you have the time.

Psychological Research

Quite a number of psychological studies report correlations between internal locus of control and desirable personal qualities. Again, note that I say "correlates," which means that these behaviors are often found together with internality—that individual Internals may or may not display these desirable behaviors, but very likely will. So, when we say that internality correlates with the more frequent use of logical thinking, we mean that most Internals will tend to think more logically than do most Externals. Furthermore, when we say that we wish that those for whom we care would learn to be more internal, we can assume that, as they do, they will also begin to think more logically.

The desirable behaviors we'll be discussing below are the result of a search through the psychological literature. Each statement is supported by at least one data-based research study, and, in some cases by extensive reviews of the research literature. In most cases, these studies are published in journals where a board of psychologists (called "juried journals") reviewed the quality of the reported research. Examples from these studies highlight some of the more impressive findings of this body of research.

For example, researchers in one study administered a test to measure the self-reported happiness of 171 university students and then administered a questionnaire to determine the students' level of internality.[1] When the scores of the students were correlated, the results showed conclusively that those who scored highly on the happiness scale also scored higher on the internality scale (see the section on "happiness," below). This research is indeed impressive, but more impressive is the fact that seven other entirely separate data-based studies have found the same result, serving to statistically and psychologically support our thesis that Internals are simply happier than Externals. The number and quality of these studies significantly increase our confidence in the judgment that Internals are happier.

Similarly, if one values school achievement, one will want to be an Internal. A large number of studies (some of them reviews of other large research studies) confirm that Internals do indeed do better in school,[2] and the sheer volume of this work, which consistently presents data that Internals have more academic success, is both significant and convincing.

Many of these studies are not simple, but well worth our attention. Consider the following study in which the investigator analyzed a large body of employment data to find (after controlling for race, educational attainment, labor market experience, and collective bargaining affiliation) that Internals clearly earn higher hourly wages than do Externals.[3] In fact, Internals are found to earn more money for the same amount of time they work and earn more across a wide variety of employment situations. This is a stunning finding, one that suggests what we all could suspect: that Internals make more desirable employees.

Armed with this information, we can appreciate that the list of desirable behaviors that correlate with the quality of being an Internal would be extensive—and it is.

This is an internet link to an online article that provides links to most of the articles cited on pages 37 to 46: *http://www. teachinternalcontrol.com/uploads/WhyTeachInternalLocusofControl. doc.pdf.*

INTERNALS ARE INDIVIDUALS WHO:

1. Experience greater personal well-being
2. Display more motivation to innovate, complete tasks, and perform well
3. Exhibit superior cognitive functioning
4. Are more successful in learning and academic achievement
5. Exhibit more desirable social and sociopolitical behavior
6. Are more successful in work and economic activities
7. Engage in healthier behaviors, are healthier, and live longer lives
8. Are generally happier in all aspects of their lives
9. Take responsibility for themselves and resist outside influences, both necessary precursors for moral behavior

Let's look at each of these internal behaviors in turn.

1. Internals experience greater personal well-being. Studies find that Internals are more confident, have higher levels of self-esteem than Externals,[4-16] and are more certain than Externals that they will succeed in tasks they undertake.[17] Several studies have found that Internals are less prone to depression and "learned helplessness," and if they do become depressed are more likely to recover sooner.[18-30] Some studies have found that Internals are less prone to suicide,[31-8] and at least 14 studies indicate that Internals experience less debilitating anxiety than Externals and are less anxious when they take tests.[39-52]

There is also evidence that Internals are more active and less impulsive than Externals[53-6] and that individuals who rate as Internals report themselves to be more assertive and are rated by others to be more assertive as well.[57] One study has reported that Internals are not only more apt to see humor in their own predicaments, but that they also seem to be more objective and detached in how they perceive themselves in general.[58-9]

Research shows that where Externals put less value on reinforcement following failure, Internals seem to accept responsibility for both success and failure, forget failure more quickly,[60-4] and react more constructively to threats.[65-6] One study concluded that Internals are more likely to engage in efforts to improve their situation,[67] and Internals have been found to respond more constructively to traumas and life changes.[68-73]

Individuals with mental illnesses and symptoms of mental illnesses, on the other hand, tend to have lower levels of internality.[74-6] For instance, Externals display more severe obsessive-compulsive symptoms than do Internals,[77] and alcoholics, especially those who are highly dependent, tend to have a more external locus of control.[78-9] Externals are more likely than Internals to manifest post-traumatic stress disorder (PTSD), even when similar environmental offenses have taken place,[80] and individuals with anorexia nervosa tend to fall on the external side of the locus of control continuum as well.[81-2] It has also been found that most personality disorders can be linked to those who demonstrate a more external locus of control,[83] and one particular study has found that those with more internality are better equipped to manage their mental disorder.[84]

Furthermore, Internals are not only less neurotic than Externals,[85] but their propensity for increased self-direction appears to lower their levels of stress and allow them to respond better to the stresses and setbacks that occur.[86-100] One study has even reported that Internals have a more positive view of the afterlife.[101]

2. Internals are more motivated to innovate, complete the tasks they start, and perform well. Internals appear to be more driving and hardworking than Externals[102-4] and locus of control was found in one study to actually predict self-determination.[105] Internals have been shown to display more motivation to do well in school, complete school, and pursue higher levels of education,[106-18] and have been shown to give up less easily on problems, use their time more efficiently than Externals,[119-26] and show greater motivation in the workforce.[127-30]

3. Internals exhibit superior cognitive functioning. Research shows us that Internals display and utilize a series of cognitive skills that, taken together, indicate a higher level of functional intelligence. Several studies indicate that Internals are apt to engage in more information seeking behavior[131-4] and are more sensitive than Externals to environmental cues.[135-8] Internals have also been shown to be more knowledgeable than Externals on topics that personally interest them. For example, prisoners who are more internal know more about parole[139] and tuberculosis patients who are more internal have more objective knowledge about the disease itself.[140] Internals are also more likely than Externals to use strategies of cognitive organization[141-3] and to make use of information when problem-solving.[144-7]

Internals are more likely to have insight,[148] more likely to use foresight in planning, and more likely to overcome learned helplessness.[149] Several studies also support the assertion that Internals are also more logical in their thought patterns, less dogmatic, and tend not to employ stereotypes in their thinking.[150-4]

Internals have greater verbal fluency,[155] better communication skills,[156-7] are reported to have better memory,[158-9] and to be more likely to improve episodic memory when provided the training to do so.[160] Internals have also been shown to be more creative in general.[161]

4. Internals are more successful learners and academic achievers. Numerous studies document the fact that Internals score higher on standardized achievement tests and other measures of academic achievement,[162-83] and profit more from instruction and training programs in reading and mathematics.

The relationship between school grades and internality is not as clear, however. Although internality does appear to interact with age and gender, and studies have found positive correlations between internality and performance grades,[184-94] other studies have shown no correlation between grades and internal control as students approach college level.[195-6] Interestingly, this lack of correlation is more marked in females, where one study reported a negative correlation for college females.[197-200] Research suggests that this lack of significant correlation may be due to the fact that internal college students do not work primarily for grades at this academic level.[201]

Several studies have found that Internals are more likely than Externals to finish college and more likely to finish their college coursework within the traditional four-year period.[202] Hence, internal locus of control is associated with success in education, and with moving on to higher education.[203-7] Internals are not only more likely to complete distance learning courses and self-instructional programmed computer courses,[208] but students with an internal locus of control are more confident in their academic abilities all around.[209]

5. Internals exhibit more desirable social and sociopolitical behavior. From a societal perspective, we find that internality is also significantly correlated with social concerns. For example, individuals with a high level of internal control seek to influence and control social situations,[210-12] often describe themselves as being assertive, and are often described by others in the same way.[213-15] A number of studies have shown that Internals seek to influence how others perceive them and are often judged as being more popular among their peers.[216-18] Internals tend to have more influence with others,[219-22] but are less aggressive;[223-6] less likely to use violence, threats, or coercion in interpersonal situations;[227-30] and more likely to be considerate of and helpful to others.[231-5] Thus, although Internals use their assertiveness to influence others, they are not disposed to being hostile or aggressive.

As children, Internals are less likely to have behavioral problems[236-7] and tend to perceive their parents as more nurturing.[238] They also respond more constructively to frustration than do Externals.[239-40] Some studies have even revealed that Internals are more likely to act ethically and less likely to be corrupt.[241-4]

Internals are also more likely to employ cautious sexual and pregnancy-related behaviors, such as consistent use of contraceptives.[245] Young women with more self-directedness are less likely to get pregnant as teenagers,[246-7] and pregnant women with an internal health locus of control are less likely to display health behaviors that are harmful to the fetus,[248] such as drug use.[249]

One prison study has shown that convicted offenders are more likely to fall on the External side of the scale;[250] another has revealed that an important factor of prisoner rehabilitation involves shifting this measurement from more external to more internal.[251] Internals also tend to have a better response to counseling and therapy than do Externals.[252-3]

Research further indicates that this pattern is much the same in sociopolitical activities, where Internals are more likely to have political and social objectives,[254-5] and tend to be less prejudiced and more politically knowledgeable.[256-8] Internals commit themselves verbally to social action as well; at least two studies have reported that they tend to be more actively engaged in direct sociopolitical action.[259-60]

We can safely say, therefore, that individuals who are more internal tend to be less hostile and aggressive toward others and to actively seek to influence their social and political environment. In a sense the efforts of Internals appear to be goal-directed, where they prefer to work to attain social objectives rather than invest in personal attacks.

Stop! Time out!

Are your eyes glazing over? Is this list of research findings overwhelming? If your answer is yes, then you are not alone. A common reaction is, "Alright already, I get it. Internals are the good guys, the superheroes, yada, yada, yada. I hear you."

But there's a reason for this foray into statistics and list making. First of all, this compilation of research findings is not like a cable channel that creates fact by repeating certain assertions over and over. No, this is a very different context. It is important to recognize that each of these studies was undertaken independently of all the other studies and it was carried out by researchers who often did not know each other, or even of each other. These are researchers who have staked their personal and professional reputations on the integrity and validity of their conclusions, and their studies are based upon different sets of data using a great variety of designs, populations, and measures spanning the country and the world for over 50 years. In most cases the studies were also reviewed by peers in the field.

That's why, with so many individually undertaken research studies resulting in statistical confirmation, one can only say that there is a uniquely strong case supporting the relationship between internality and desirable behaviors throughout the spectrum of human behavior. And there is no longer any doubt that if we increase our internality by learning to be more internal we will experience a major shift in the quality of our life.

Go! Time in.

---

6. Internals are more successful at work and at other money-related activities. When we're talking about career success, we can easily see that being more internal would be a bonus. In fact, it has been found that internality is beneficial both at work and relative to other kinds of economic pursuits.[261] Even in circumstances where an internal locus of control has not been linked to academic success,[262] it still remains correlated to money matters and success. For example, in several studies internality has been associated with making better choices concerning career and with the overall success of whatever career has been chosen.[263-6]

Why would this be the case? One reason could be that workers with higher levels of internality tend to be more efficient and more reliable,[267-72] whereas those with higher levels of externality reveal a tendency toward poorer overall work performance.[273-4] One good example is farmers who, when more internal, tend to be more efficient[275] and more prone to working styles that promote safety.[276-7] It also makes sense that Internals are more likely to be driven by intrinsic reward,[278-80] and quicker to rejoin the workforce if they've had to leave due to an injury.[281]

Internality is associated with higher rates of employment,[282-4] better money management,[285-6] and greater levels of job satisfaction,[287-93] and is considered an essential element of the constellation of traits that create successful entrepreneurs.[294-7]

Internals have been shown to earn higher wages,[298-301] even after controlling for other relevant variables, such as education, ethnicity, and experience,[302] and a shift from more externality to more internality has been associated with a getting a promotion at work.[303]It is worth noting as well that although the causation could go either way, individuals from lower socioeconomic circumstances tend to have less internality.[304-6]

7. Internals engage in healthier behavior, are healthier, and live longer lives. What better reason could there be for raising our level of internality than knowing how it could make us healthier and happier? Studies have indeed found that being more internal directly correlates to better physical health,[307-11] including a reduced disposition toward chronic headache,[312-13] reduced rates of obesity,[314-15] and a reduced risk for high blood pressure.[316-17] One study has shown that Internals have a better physical response to stress, as characterized by less brain atrophy in a specific region of the brain known as the hippocampus.[318]

Furthermore, when we are more internal in outlook, we are more likely to rate good health as something that is important and to exhibit more health-conscious behaviors.[319-25] Hence, Internals have been shown to experience fewer addiction problems related to alcohol[326-7] and cigarettes.[328-30]

Not only do Internals have generally healthier, more constructive reactions to illness,[331-40] they tend to have better prognoses when diagnosed with chronic diseases;[341-4] adhere more effectively to medication regimens and their doctor's advice;[345-6] and respond better to treatment.[347-50] Amazingly, some studies have even shown that, when combined with other factors, Internals also have a reduced risk of mortality[351-2] compared to Externals who reveal an increased risk.[353-4]

8. Internals are happier people. We learned earlier that Internals tend to have reduced rates of depression and other mental illnesses. Therefore, it makes sense that they would also tend to be just plain happier. This tendency translates into the fact that Internals experience fewer negative life events[355] and an overall better quality of life and greater life satisfaction than their external counterparts.[356-62]

Several factors that promote happiness can be linked directly to one's measurement on the internality scale. For example, internality has been shown to be important in pursuit of goals that are essential for life satisfaction and happiness, such as commitment to family and friends,[363] and to weaken the relationship between materialism and unhappiness.[364] Studies that measure happiness specifically[365-9] have found that internality is directly related to positive affect,[370] emotional well-being,[371] and overall contentment.[372]

9. Internals take responsibility and resist outside influences, both necessary precursors for moral behavior. Some studies show that Internals are more likely than Externals to resist conformity.[373-7] For instance, having higher levels of internal locus of control has been shown to be an important factor for former gang members who attempt to disengage from gang life.[378] We also know that the tendency to conform comes in many shapes and sizes as born out by the studies showing that Internals are less responsive to advertisements than Externals.[379] In an interesting twist, Internals also generally feel more resistance to conformity due to a deep commitment to self-generated principles, argued to be essential elements of moral reasoning.[380]

Internals have also been found to be more satisfied with their superiors.[381] One reason for this seeming discrepancy may be that Internals tend to more actively seek superiors for whom they can comfortably work. Internality is also one of several traits that has been shown to contribute to more ethical behavior in the workplace.[382]

Socially responsible behavior is something often promoted by Internals.[383] A disregard for responsibility, on the other hand, has been found to be one of the main correlates of an external outlook.[384] Although possibly situational, studies also suggest that Internals are less likely to cheat as well.[385-6]

Internality, You, and Your Children

When I read J. S. Coleman's landmark national study entitled "Equality of Educational Opportunity," (the one that analyzed the achievement records of 150,000 pupils), one finding jumped out at me. Coleman and his associates state, "A pupil attitude factor, which appears to have a stronger relationship to achievement than do all the 'school' factors taken together, is the extent to which an individual feels that he has control over his own destiny." I believe what Coleman and his associates mean by this statement is that internality alone has a greater effect on a student's achievement than the quality of teaching, the curriculum, the classroom size, the amount of money spent per student, the school (public or private), the school organization, and the level of teacher skill and dedication all put together.

Coleman and his associates also state, "The child's sense of control of his environment is most strongly related to achievement." If it is true that a child's sense of control overrides all family variables and all school variables, then it also overrides race, social class, economic level, and gender as well! Hence, internality is more significant than whether we are white and a northerner or black and a southerner, whether we are middle class and live in the suburbs or are economically deprived and live in the inner city. If you have a certain degree of internality—if you have "IT"—you will achieve in the school setting.

What this landmark survey of schools clearly shows us is that:

The single most important thing you can do to enable your children to successfully achieve in school is to teach them to become Internals.

The single most important thing *you* can do to successfully achieve in your academic endeavors is to be an Internal.

Internality: An Educational Policy Imperative

Again I turn to J. S. Coleman's landmark study in which he concludes:

"Taking all these results together, one implication stands out above all: That schools bring little influence to bear on a child's achievement that is independent of his background and general social context; and this very lack of an independent effect means that the inequalities imposed on children by their home, neighborhood, and peer environment are carried along to become the inequalities with which they confront adult life at the end of school. For equality of educational opportunity through the schools must imply a strong effect of the schools that is independent of the child's immediate social environment, and that strong independent effect is not present in American schools."

Do you feel as discouraged as I did when I read Coleman's statement? Is there nothing we can do that can have "a strong independent effect" on the ability of our children to achieve success in school?

As I write these words, the school superintendent of Washington D.C. is engaged in a war with the teachers of her district. The superintendent is holding the teachers accountable for the lack of student achievement. Her thinking likely sounds something like this:

If she could only get rid of the poor teachers and bring in all "Teach America-like" candidates, then her children would achieve.

But Coleman's data indicates this is not the reality; that though teachers *can* make a difference, they can't make all that much difference. Experienced teachers know in their guts that although they may be able to change learner achievement to a degree, there are definite limits to their influence. This is one reason that they look askance at proposals to link their compensation to student learning measures. Coleman's data clearly shows that student background and social context rule the extent of pupil achievement, and that teachers have a marginal effect on learner achievement.

Also, as I write these words charter schools are the rage, based on the belief that they improve student achievement and, in doing so, put pressure on public schools, provide competition, and force the public schools to change. Hmm...so, school factors and school organizational attributes will improve student achievement? Not according to Coleman's data, which found that school organization factors have very little effect on achievement. Unsurprisingly, data is now slowly accumulating that shows that there are *no* differences between the achievement of children in charter schools and those in public schools.[387] In fact, at worst, there is growing evidence that economically deprived children do even more poorly in charter schools[ibid.] and are, in effect, being shortchanged in charter school environments.

So now we ask, "Is there nothing we can do to be more effective? Are there no clues in Coleman's findings that might suggest something that might be done?"

Wait a minute...let's look at something else Coleman said just before the words we quoted above: "Attitudes, such as a sense of control of the environment or a belief in the responsiveness of the environment, are highly related to achievement, but appear to be little influenced by variations in school characteristics."

In essence, Coleman is saying that he found that belief in internal control is *highly related to achievement*, but that schools have little influence on this variable.

Can such an outcome be changed? Is it possible for schools to focus on the nature of their students' "attitudes" in order to increase their levels of internality and thereby increase their achievement? Wouldn't this change the lives of children and effectively offer a truly equal educational opportunity to all our youth?

Why haven't educational policy leaders focused like a laser on these potential attitudinal shifts? Why haven't they demanded that we make provisions at every level and in multiple venues to impact this variable, one which so clearly has the possibility of a significant payoff?

Frankly, it's a mystery.

It's a mystery that the National Institute of Education has not commissioned research to explore this possibility, and a mystery that we are not pouring resources into studying how to affect this critical attitude.

Is it because the policy poobahs don't think you can teach children belief in internal locus of control?

Perhaps.

. . .

In the following chapters we will share EXACTLY how you can teach internal control to others.

Chapter 3

Teach Internal Locus of Control by Teaching a Personal Achievement Strategy

Directly put:

We teach Internal control by teaching a Personal Achievement Strategy™.

When we teach learners a Personal Achievement Strategy, learners experience increasing personal achievement.

As learners experience increasing personal achievement, they increasingly believe that they can influence the course of their life.

This increase in learner belief in their ability to control their life in turn leads to increasing achievement which in turn leads to an increasing sense of internal control.

This is the upward spiral we seek:

achievement > increased belief in internal control > increasing achievement > increasing belief in internal locus of control >

We teach achievement behavior by teaching a six-step personally oriented achievement strategy. This six-step personal achievement strategy is based on research about achievement and about belief in the idea of internal control. We teach this six-step strategy by having learners: (1) study themselves; (2) create goal ideas; (3) set personal goals; (4) plan; (5) strive to achieve these same self-set goals; and (6) evaluate the effectiveness of their efforts.

In using this personal achievement strategy to achieve personal goals, learners act and think like Internals. As strategy users repeatedly act and think like Internals and experience achievement, they come to believe in their ability to influence their life. They become Internals!

Suppose someone were to come to you and say that she believes in the value of being an Internal. She then asks you, "How should I act to be internal?" What would you tell her to do? My answer would be to learn to use this six-step verbal self-mediating Personal Achievement Strategy because it is the operational definition, the cookbook answer, to the question, "How should I act to influence the course of my life?"

Teaching internal locus of control by teaching a Personal Achievement Strategy is supported by the research we have discussed in the first chapter that shows that achievement and internal locus of control are interactive and that in many cases achievement leads to a greater belief in internal control. In effect we are initiating the upward spiral of **achievement> internal control> achievement>** by teaching achievement behavior, which in turn increases belief in internal locus of control. This is the defining hypothesis underlying our method of teaching internality.

More About the Strategy

Now let's look more closely at the Personal Achievement Strategy. In developing instructional materials for fifth-grade students we created the visual below (see Figure 3). As you can see, each step of the strategy is illustrated with a figure to indicate the sequential relationship of each step to the next, and then suggests a repeating circular motion. In our programs we used this visualization again and again as a memory device to key learners to the kind of activity in which they were engaged and to help them remember the strategy as a whole.

Figure 3: The Personal Achievement Strategy™

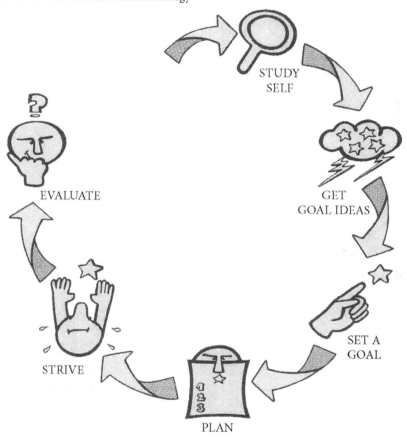

STUDY
SELF

GET
GOAL IDEAS

SET A
GOAL

PLAN

STRIVE

EVALUATE

A second visualization of the personal achievement strategy can be seen below in Figure 4. Note the activities listed under each step. These activities describe the behaviors that are a concomitant part of each step and might be thought of as sub-skills of each step. These activities were introduced over time in our instructional program in different rounds of utilizing the strategy™.

Figure 4: The Personal Achievement Strategy™ with associated skills.

1. STUDY SELF	**2. GET GOAL IDEAS**	**3. SET A GOAL**
• Recall Past Achievements • Survey Strengths	• Focus on Strengths and Achievements • Brainstorm	• Possible • Specific in Time, Quantity, and Kind • Medium Risk
4. PLAN	**5. STRIVE**	**6. EVALUATE**
• Name and Order Tasks • Question Plan • Replan	• Envision Achievement • Recall Heroes • Use Competition	• Did I get my goal? • What did I do well? • What could I improve? • How did I use the six steps?

Ideally individuals learn to use these bethaviors and incorporate them into many aspects of their day-to-day life. There are many examples; list making is an obvious one. Do you make lists of things to do? If you do, you are planning, taking control of your behavior and of your life. As you do, you are projecting a belief in internal control relative to yourself and your environment. Doesn't everyone make lists? Absolutely not! Many people do not. Frankly, if you are reading this book then there is a good chance that you are one of the ones who do—and are probably more of an Internal. But large groups of the population do not make lists.

Setting goals is another example. Many people consciously set goals. Some people set daily goals, but many set no goals at all. They simply show up for work or school and have others set out their tasks and schedules. Those who do set goals are acting internally; those who do not do so are exhibiting external behavior. These achievement behaviors can become the way in which individuals direct and control their lives.

Please note the following six critical characteristics of the Personal Achievement Strategy™.

1. The strategy is *verbally self-mediating*. Note that the steps are stated as directions and that these directions are directed to the individual using the strategy. The user guides his behavior by remembering and saying to himself, "Verbal self-mediation is a key to exerting internal control. This is how I take conscious or 'executive' control of myself, how I can modulate my feelings,[1-3] and how I can direct and control my behavior."[4-7] Consequently, the Internal personal achievement Strategy is not directed to teachers, or parents, or therapists; it is directed personally, to the user.

2. The strategy is *usable*. We have worked with fifth graders again and again as they used the strategy to achieve their goals. In doing so we observed them closely and made repeated adjustments to make this strategy more usable.[8] This strategy works! Fifth graders have successfully used it. Anyone operating at or above a fifth-grade level of chronological intelligence is able to use the strategy successfully.

3. The strategy is *self-reinforcing*. As learners use the strategy to set and achieve their own goals they become engaged and excited. They often experience the internal thrill and the satisfaction of achievement and accomplishment. And of course their achievement is often recognized and rewarded by others. The magnitude and repetition of these reinforcements build over time. They increasingly motivate learners to continue to use the strategy and to address the world as individuals who believe they have influence on their life. Again, this is the upward spiral of **achievement > belief in internal control**.

4. The strategy is *widely applicable*. This strategy is general enough that it allows users to apply it in a range of areas, or domains. We encouraged the fifth graders in our study to apply the strategy in five different domains: athletics, crafts, academics, artistic endeavors, and interpersonal relationships. However, it has been proven that this strategy can easily be applied in even wider and more sophisticated arenas, such as behaviors around health and economics.

The fifth graders were taken by the idea that they could use this strategy in their interpersonal relationships, in "making and keeping friends," as they stated it. Some used it to think about improving their athletic skills and others applied it to craft projects. What we know is that it can be used in any aspect of life. I even know people who apply variations of the strategy to enhance their spiritual growth.

5. The strategy *addresses and manages the emotional dimensions of personal behavior*. I believe this is a unique aspect of this strategy. We seek and engage emotion because it is a central component of motivation, energy, and action. For example, in the first step of the strategy we immediately begin to generate positive emotion by having learners remember past achievements. In the Striving Step we introduce and rehearse ways of managing one's will and one's motivation to work. Each step has an emotional dimension that contributes to energetic and purposeful action.

6. The strategy is *easy to understand*. I'll bet that you understood the basis for the Personal Achievement Strategy almost immediately, right? And now you can use it at a reasonable level of competence. You might benefit from some guidance in setting medium-risk, doable goals, getting goal ideas, and so on, but otherwise you can probably use this strategy in your life *right now*.

The Six Steps

At this point I believe it will help us better understand the Personal Achievement Strategy if we look more closely at each step. In doing so, I need to remind you that we developed this strategy to teach fifth graders. Accordingly, our language and our examples reference fifth graders. We depend on you to see how the strategy can apply to your life and to the lives of those that you might wish to teach.

Step 1: Studying Self. We consider this first step to be the basis on which the whole strategy stands. This step generates the ideas and feelings that make the Personal Achievement Strategy "internal" and personal. It generates the information with which the user works throughout the entire strategy. You could say that this self-knowledge is the lodestar, the guide and the inspiration of an individual's use of the Personal Achievement Strategy.

Users are asked to: (1) recall and describe their personal past achievements, (2) identify their current strengths, and (3) name their interests. They are asked to identify their feelings, judgments, and beliefs about themselves. In working with children, we issued journals designed for recording their thoughts about their strengths and achievements in words and drawings and to aid them in remembering what they think and feel.[9] The self-knowledge recorded in this first step becomes the cognitive ground and emotional energy for personal internally directed action in the steps that follow.

It is impossible to exaggerate the effect that this self-investigation had upon the children with whom we worked. For some it was the first time that they had thought of themselves in any positive way. They seemed to know their weaknesses and failures, but were seldom able to be articulate about their strengths. For many it was the first time they had been encouraged to think and talk about themselves in school. For all, it was a thoroughly absorbing and energizing experience.

In order to stimulate and inspire learners to continue to study themselves, we progressed through several different questions, including naming and listing personal strengths. In addition, we had the learners list past accomplishments and achievements. We also recommended having learners list their interests. Appropriately for fifth graders, we had the learners make charts, interrelate strengths and interests, and engage in other activities designed to build feelings of empowerment and expectations for future achievement.

We did not address problems or failures that learners might have felt needed improvement. We avoided problems because we did not want to introduce negative emotion. Instead, we found that it was always possible to deal with problem areas by reformulating them into positive goals. For example, if a learner were having a problem achieving in mathematics, we helped him formulate a specific positive goal in math. We found it easy and effective to "flip" problem statements into positive goal statements.

For fun and stimulation we supplied mirrors to the fifth graders and asked them to study themselves in the mirror for homework over a period of a day or so. We asked them to list their past achievements on the border of the mirror as they did so. Here are some actual samples of their work (see Figure 5).

Figure 5: Mirroring past achievements.

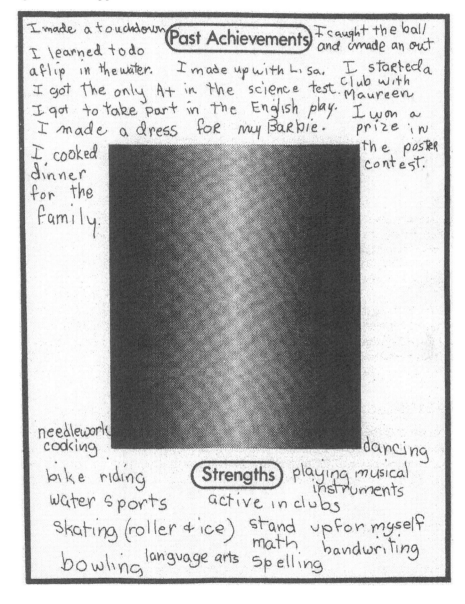

I made a touchdown **Past Achievements** I caught the ball
I learned to do
a flip in the water. I made up with Lisa. I started a
I got the only A+ in the science test. Club with
I got to take part in the English play. Maureen
I made a dress for my Barbie. prize in
I cooked the poster
dinner contest.
for the
family.

needlework
cooking dancing
bike riding **Strengths** playing musical
water sports active in clubs instruments
skating (roller & ice) stand up for myself
bowling language arts math handwriting
spelling

By asking these learners to name their past achievements we were asking them to:

- Define examples of specific personal past achievements, encouraging them to think of themselves as achievers;
- Begin to think like "doers" who set and achieve goals;
- Share their perceived achievements with others and be recognized and reinforced for their self-identified achievements; and
- Create a reservoir of personal past achievements that begins to define them in their own mind as being influential in the direction of their life; in other words, to begin to think as Internals do.

By having learners name achievements, strengths, and interests, we are building the foundation for a move to belief in internal control.

Building the foundation for internality

If you want to fully understand the power of this step you cannot do so just by reading about it; you need to try it. I would warrant that you, like most people, can identify your failings, but can you inventory your strengths as easily? Try it. Set aside some time and develop a list of past achievements. Consider different time frames, perhaps only those achievements for the past week or year. Or maybe you're more interested in trying to develop a list of major life achievements from the past. Ask yourself what others would say are your achievements. When you are satisfied, take some additional time to restate these past achievements in an easily understandable format. Finally, put this list of past achievements in a place where you can see it

---

easily and often. Feel the change in how you feel! Feel the energy!

Many personal self-growth educational programs establish the study of self as the primary object of their effort. These programs encourage discussion of feelings and self-perception as ends in themselves. We do not. We believe that internally controlled actions do not occur unless these feelings are channeled into purposeful action. The expression of emotion must be goal-channeled if it is to be anything other than an aesthetic experience: enjoyable in it's own right, but fleeting. Self-study is not the end we seek, but the beginning, the initiating fount of action for becoming internally directed. And, by the way, those who score as Internals have been found to have more personal knowledge about themselves. So, by engaging in these self-study exercises we are creating and reinforcing the subjective experience of being of an Internal.

Step 2: Getting Goal Ideas. In this second step users begin to utilize the self-information generated in the first step. Who they are, their strengths, and their interests are all "sources" for suggestions regarding what they wish to pursue. Originally we thought we could go directly to goal setting and skip this activity, but decided to introduce this step after we found that large numbers of children simply had no idea of how to be imaginative and inventive in expanding their vistas. The distressingly frequent reaction to the opportunity to choose a goal, which comes in the next step of the strategy, was, "I don't know what I want to do." This was not true of all children, of course, but the difficulty for many was further corroborated as we watched the children abandon realities about themselves and flee into meaningless choices of goals that might gain adult approval or the approbation of their peers.

Hence, our strategy calls for conscious divergent thinking about potential personal goals. It is operationally necessary in order for the strategy user to move to the next phase of goal setting. In order to make this move, we realized that we needed to teach skills for enriching and expanding the individual's goals.

In order to help the children we introduced three activities:

1. **Brainstorming.** First we had the children individually put down whatever came to mind without judgment and then join in a group to share ideas and generate more ideas.

2. **Taking inventory.** In order to broaden the children's goal setting we developed an interest inventory based on the five activity areas of Kagan and Moss (1962).[10]

3. **Fantasizing.** We introduced a variation of directed fantasizing in which the children were led in making new connections between their strengths and achievements. The intended product of this step is a list of reasonably achievable "felt" goal ideas rooted in the personal life of the user.

Reinforcing belief in internal control

A broader effect of generating goal ideas is to reinforce the feelings, perception, and expectation of the learner that he can have control over his life. When learners begin to address their universe with the questions, "What shall I decide to achieve?" and "What shall I invest my energy and commitment in doing?" they are exhibiting a belief in internal control. More, they are laying the groundwork for the significant commitment to act, and to direct the course of their life. This is in sharp contrast to the world view of the External who is lying back trying to avoid difficulties, reacting to other forces, and avoiding past failures.

Engaging in Step 2, Getting Goal Ideas, helps learners:

- Continue to generate positive energy and enthusiasm;
- Enlarge and reinforce their belief that they are actors and agents who can give direction to their lives; and
- Lay the groundwork for immediate and future commitment to meaningful personal goals.

In other words, learners are now ready to set a goal.

Step 3: Setting a Goal.[11-12] This step gets down to the business of choosing a goal. It requires the learner to formulate a goal simply and clearly, judging it for (1) possibility, (2) specificity, and (3) medium risk, based on give directions provided on meeting these criteria. "Possibility" indicates that the goal should be controllable and fall within a reasonable range of expectation. "Growing to be a 7-foot-tall basketball player" is not controllable or "doable," but "making five consecutive baskets from six feet out" is. "Specificity" means that the goal should be delineated in (a) kind, (b) quality, and (c) time needed for attainment. "Swimming" is not an acceptable statement, but to "swim 20 lengths using my best stroke by the end of the month" is. "Medium risk" encourages the learner to choose a goal of 40 to 60% difficulty, a level that should challenge, but not overtax or under-tax the learner's abilities.

Again, the learner should be seeking to control his behavior by setting a goal that is doable. He is taking responsibility for the effectiveness of his behavior only if he thinks he can do it. This is the point of commitment. Do the strategy users really want to achieve their goal? Do they really feel that can do it? Are they energetically and consciously taking responsibility for doing it?

Externals do not commit. They do not set specific or doable goals. They do not get specific about quality or number. Often they set goals that are too high or too low in risk. These actions protect them from commitment and from putting themselves on the line to "get it done."

Consider the example of an inner city boy who, when asked what he hoped to become, said that he wanted to a brain surgeon or a star baseball player. Yes, laudatory, but these goals are unrealistic in that they were long range, and an example of what can be called "magical thinking,"[13] where wishing will make it so. Poverty-level adolescent girls had a tendency toward similar desirable goals (remember, this was the 1970s) as well—a nice house, a reasonable family, a stable parental relationship, as well as careers as lawyers or scientists. Yes, these are all things we recognize as desirable and healthy, but without an idea of what to do to move toward these objectives—without a plan, a next step, an idea of what to do this coming week to move toward their hopes—these goals will likely not have been achieved. What these wishes required was the achievement of a long series of small discrete steps, steps that built on the attainment of prior goals.

In our instructions to the children, we provided examples of other children setting goals, and we asked them to discriminate goals that did and did not meet the above criteria. We also provided practice in rewriting goals. Finally, we called upon the children to formulate and critique their own personal goals. Our experience showed that goal-setting skills are difficult to teach, but our evaluation data showed conclusively that the fifth-grade children were able to learn these skills and that they did apply them.

Successful goal setting

Internals are better able to predict goal levels that they can attain. They try and learn to set realistic goal levels, as shown in several laboratory studies.[14] This is very important as it is one way to gain a sense of control. When we are realistic in formulating and setting goals we have a much greater probability of achievement. As pointed out earlier, it is from successfully setting goals and achieving them that we begin to gain a sense of control...which in turn leads to continuing to **setting realistic goals > the upward spiral**.

As you'll see in the next chapter, we were successful in teaching children to set more realistic goals. You can learn to teach this crucial skill as well.

Step 4: Planning. Internals are process-conscious. They know how to plan and how to ask nuts-and-bolts questions about available resources and the necessary steps to achieve their goals. In Step 4, Internals use the specific and controllable goals derived in the last step to build a workable plan. "Planning" is defined as naming and ordering tasks. In our work with children, we learned that they (like adults) really do know how to cognitively plan for reaching goals, but they usually fail to do the planning. For example, while many individuals know how to create personal budget plans, few actually do it. Internals are the ones who get it done.[15]

Making the transfer from knowing how to plan to actually doing and getting real-life feedback on the value of planning is essential to becoming and continuing to be an Internal. In our instruction we defined effective planning behavior as:

- Listing tasks to be done to reach goals;
- Sequencing tasks to be done to reach goals;
- Matching tasks with resources available;
- Collecting necessary information and re-planning as necessary;
- Selecting needed work techniques; and
- Seeking help when needed.

Let's take typical situation, such as taking a driving trip. If your goal is to take a two-week car trip to Arizona from Maine, you need to plan how long it will take to get there, where you'll stay, how you'll eat, and how much it will cost. The more you plan the better chance there is that you will have a positive and satisfying experience, and planning is reinforced by the greater probably of success. In this situation, Externals might drive off with little or no preparation, run out of time and/or money, and have to rush back.

Failing to plan often reminds us that we should have invested more effort in planning. Not all goals need plans the way complicated ones do, however. One of the examples we use in our instructional materials asks our learners to distinguish between catching a frog by a stream and catching a frog when one lives in the center of the city. The message: goals for which we plan are bigger and more complicated.

Planning further cements commitment and intention. It creates a sense of committing to act into the environment, and it precipitates purposeful action. Plan and you are ready to work your plan. You clearly see the next step. This is no longer magical thinking. You are ready to work toward your goal.

Step 5: Striving. Okay, so now learners have their goal and their plan. The next step is to do it—just do it! This step delivers two messages. The first is simple, but profound: Things do not just happen. They require work. They often require hard and persistent effort. If you want to achieve your goals, you must work! The second message is that a person can internally control his ability to begin, to work hard, and to persist at a task; he need not submit to the whim of how he feels at any one moment. Learners are taught that they can "prime" themselves to generate more energy, work hard, and persist by using strategies that work quite well, such as:

- Making a public commitment;
- Remembering and focusing on past successes;
- Imagining what it will feel like to achieve your goal;
- Recalling heroes who have persisted to achieve goals (a particularly effective tool for the fifth graders with whom we were working); and
- Competing with one's own past record, head to head with other people, or with one's own standard of excellence.

We need to deliver the idea that things don't happen by themselves, and that it can be difficult to achieve a goal. Everyone must learn to work, but there are many examples of things people do to help themselves persist. I am sure you have a few that work for you. The point is that Internals refuse to have the level of their efforts governed by their moods. They talk to themselves and coach themselves to strive. They persist in being cognitively and emotionally in control of their work effort.

Step 6: Evaluating. This is the last step of our Personal Achievement Strategy. Internals are very sensitive to the results of their efforts. They want to know how well they did, and there is evidence that they do not accept contrived or false praise. They *really* want to know how well they did—even if the news is not good—and they prefer encouragement to praise.[16] In this strategy step the user determines the quality of his goal achievement. There are no outside authorities to make this evaluation or judgment. In keeping with the concept of internality, each person is responsible for evaluating him- or herself. In effect, the user is led to hold himself responsible for the effectiveness of his behavior. This is a key aspect of internality.

We encouraged users to make a specific determination: "Did I achieve my goal, yes or no?" If they succeeded we wanted them to savor their success. This is important reinforcement. We wanted them to feel good! If they did not succeed we wanted them to feel bad because feeling bad can also be a potential source of energy. Since feeling bad is uncomfortable, we can learn to utilize this feeling to motivate ourselves in future efforts. Unfortunately, friends and parents sometimes rob us of this energy source by helping the user make excuses. That is why we do not stop there.

We teach Personal Achievement Strategy users three primary questions to evaluate their efforts:

1. Did I achieve my goal as I have specified it?
2. What did I do well?; What can I improve?
3. Did I use the strategy effectively?

Summary

In this step, we ask users to evaluate their efforts and learn from them. We address success and failure in a constructive manner. If they have failed and feel badly then here is something they can do: analyze their performance and resolve to do better next time. "Next time I will start sooner. Next time I will set a lower goal and ask for help." Users reduce their anxiety and depression, faces the future, and think through how to do better.

If the users have done well, we should be sure to be clear about what things they did to succeed and remember them for the next time.

We were successful in teaching children to use these questions to evaluate their use of the Personal Achievement Strategy™.

The Personal Achievement Strategy as a Whole

As our strategy progresses, the steps flow one into another until the originally set goal is or is not achieved. The experience of using the strategy creates energy and produces enlightening information for the next round of setting and seeking to achieve one's goal. As the users continue using the Personal Achievement Strategy in their lives, they become more skillful in its use. The strategy and the specific steps can and do become habits of address, attitude, and action in the individuals' daily lives. These individuals not only come to believe in internal control, but act in a way that puts them in control.

I know people who get up each morning and write out their goals for the day. Then, at day's end, they review their success in attaining these goals, crossing out the ones they have achieved and discard ing others, or resetting goals that they did not attain. I know other people who periodically take time out to rethink their intermediate-range interests and generate goal ideas. They actually write out their goal ideas and keep them available for routine reference. I know people who have worked out routines to help themselves focus and work or, as we say, strive. Often they have tricks they use to energize and to goad themselves into "getting it done." These individuals are invariably high achievers, and are very able and successful people.

Do you know people like this? Probably. They are Internals. Can these behaviors be taught? Can you learn these behaviors? You know you can. Do you want to teach your children...your students...your employees these behaviors? I hope so.

At first, the use of the Personal Achievement Strategy tends to feel somewhat rigid, mechanical, and inflexible. But with practice its users naturally become more flexible, at times even eclectic in their application of the strategy as they repeatedly practice using it in an increasing range of situations. I compare it to learning a physical skill, let's say touch typing or dancing. At first you mechanically try to follow a verbal set of self directions; in the case of dancing, one, two, slide-step-slide, and so on. You walk stiffly and attempt to be correctly square in your movements, at first hesitant and tight. But with practice, you are able to concentrate on the music, be more flexible, more skillful, and more interpretive. You can show your style…be the graceful gliding person you really are. Eventually you can enjoy yourself.

So it is with the use of Personal Achievement Strategy. Through practice and use learners become skilled in setting doable goals of medium risk, specific in time, kind, and number. They find themselves to be quicker and the experience to be less laborious. Soon, setting doable medium-risk goals simply becomes a part of their ongoing behavior. I am sure you have had any number of experiences like this in learning the many useful skills of life.

Research suggests that we can acquire a motor habit, such as tying our shoes in a different way (psychologists think up the most annoying activities, don't they?) by engaging in about 11 or 12 repetitions. Athletes practice "reps" all the time to learn and then make new behavior patterns part of their habitual behavior. We, too, can acquire the use of the internal control pattern of behavior through repeated repetition, laborious and awkward at first, but soon to become an easily usable tool in day-to-day life. If you wish to become an Internal, this is a way to do it.

An Analogy: Problem Solving

Let's examine a similar strategy to help clarify and illustrate what we mean. Suppose we wanted to teach "belief in the value of systematic problem solving." We could do so by presenting testimonials and examples and subjecting our learners to lectures. We could require them to take a test on the definition of problem thinking. Both are traditional approaches. But though the end product would be knowledge about problem solving, it would be a conceptual understanding only; learners would not have learned how to use a problem-solving approach. They would not have internalized it, taken it in. They would be left on their own to utilize these behaviors if they so chose.

Another way to teach "belief in the value of problem solving" is to teach learners *to use* the systematic problem-solving method to address problems of interest to them; to teach learners to act like problem solvers. But first we need to define the behaviors understood to be problem thinking. And guess what? The literature is in agreement that the systematic problem-solving method can be described as having six sequential behavior steps that recycle. Yes, six steps—just as the Personal Achievement Strategy has six steps. I am sure you will recognize them:

1. Define the problem
2. Analyze the problem
3. Generate possible solutions
4. Analyze the solutions
5. Select the best solution(s)
6. Plan the next course of action (next steps)

We might assume that as we taught our learners to use this behavioral strategy to solve problems of interest to themselves they would begin to "believe in the value" of the problem-solving method. Indeed, utilizing the method itself requires just such a belief. Therefore, we believe that the application of the strategy would be a good way to teach "belief" in the method. But more, much more than that, we will also have taught the learners to *be* problem solvers. Teaching the use of the problem-solving method is in and of itself a wonderful accomplishment.

Some engineering schools emphasize this mindset throughout their entire program where they seek to train their graduates to be and act as problem solvers. This gives us the infamous mindset of the engineer that results in that sometimes heard comment, "Oh, he's an engineer…you know how they think." To me this is a triumph of an educational program and an effective way of thinking. For example, one of my sons is a tool and die maker. He can fix all sorts of things like lawn mowers and such. It is clear to me that he approaches problems around my house in a very different and much more effective way than I do, and I welcome this engineering mindset.

And so it is with being an Internal. We need to define the strategy and teach the learners to use it to set and achieve their own goals. They will come to believe in internal control. They will be able to act and think as Internals think. They will be Internals.

Operational Arguments for Using This Strategy

After addressing the theoretical value and validity of using this strategy to teach internal control, I would like to state the positive operational reasons to utilize this six-step Personal Achievement Strategy. The strategy:

- Is easy to understand;
- Is easy to explain;
- Is easy to remember;
- Is fun for children;
- Results in achievement experiences;
- Offers a behavioral description of internal control;
- Manages and utilizes the emotional and attitudinal dimensions of behavior and experience;
- Is applicable in many areas of life;
- Utilizes the power of verbal self-mediation of behavior;
- Can be incorporated in whole or in part to one's daily behavior;
- Puts the learner/user in control, consistent with internal control behavior;

- Flows from one step to another, from one goal to another;
- Generates a "belief" in internal control; and
- Is scientifically validated (see next chapter).

I believe this book offers support for the teaching and use of the Personal Achievement Strategy to teach internal control. The final and most persuasive validation, however, will come from your personal use of the strategy, your gut check. Try it. Try to use it, or parts of it, in your life. Does it begin to provide you with a greater sense of control? If so, then you will know it works in a very personal way!

. . .

Now we leave rhetoric, logic, and opinion behind. In the next chapter we will look at a large scale scientifically structured field study validating the effectiveness of teaching this Personal Achievement Strategy to dispose learners to become Internals.

Chapter 4

Teach Internal Control:
A Validating Field Test and Evaluation

The Questions

Before we charge into learning to teach Internality by teaching achievement behavior, we need to make sure we know the answer to the question: "Will this really work?"

If we teach learners this six-step Personal Achievement Strategy, will our learners learn to be Internals? Will learners significantly increase their belief in internal control? Will they exhibit the behaviors that are associated with internal control? Will they exhibit these behaviors in their day-to-day lives?

The answer for all these questions is: Yes, yes, yes, and yes.

How do I know? Through the same kind of research we talked about in Chapter 2. Let's discuss that research here in detail.

The field study

In summary, my colleagues and I created a programmed multimedia instructional package for use with children in the fifth, sixth, and seventh grades. Our objectives were to teach a six-step strategy for setting and achieving personally meaningful goals and to develop attitudes that would dispose the children to use the same strategy in their lives. This instructional program was field tested in 1972–73 with three groups of fifth-grade students from 99 classrooms in 30 schools in the Philadelphia area: the treatment group, students participating in the Achievement Competency Training program (hereafter referred to as ACT), the comparison group, students participating in a comparison curriculum, and students who received no instruction. Three classes within each school were randomly assigned to each of the three treatment groups.

What we found when we measured the students' performance in this considerable field test was enormously satisfying because those students who received instruction in utilizing the strategy of personal achievement increased in internality in several different ways. In fact, compared with students in the other groups, these students showed:

- Greater belief in internal control of behavior;
- Greater tendency to prescribe self-directed solutions to problems;
- Less of a discrepancy between self-predicted performance and self-set standards of good performance;
- More realistic personal standards for good performance; and
- Use of the Personal Achievement Strategy in their daily life situations and more.

The evidence is persuasive: we were successful in teaching the behavior of internal control and a belief in the quality of internal control.

. . .

Before we continue, a word about the organization of the remainder of this chapter. We have begun with a brief overview of our field test and evaluation. Such a brief report or abstract is not adequate for most readers who will want to have a better idea of how these results were determined. Consequently, we have described how we arrived at these result in greater detail in the remainder of this chapter. This description is aimed at a fairly knowledgeable general audience and should be satisfactory for most readers. On the other hand, if you are interested in reviewing more research specifics, such as the mathematical design and analysis of the evaluation data or copies of the measures used in our assessment, you can access this information in two other documents. These documents are cited in this chapter's endnote references and will be accessible online at teachinternalcontrol.com.

Also, please note that many of the words and ideas that follow have been taken from the evaluation report written by Barbara Brandes, Ph.D., the program's evaluator.

What follows is a report of the field trial evaluation for you to skim or study; it's your choice.

Why fifth graders?

You may be wondering why we selected fifth-grade students to test the efficacy of this locus of control strategy. There are three reasons for our decision: (1) because development psychologists tell us that fifth graders are the youngest age at which children are cognitively able to use a behavioral strategy;[1] (2) because we planned to develop and use instructional materials that assumed the learners could read at or about the 3.5 grade level, or about the level needed to read simple directions; and (3) because we assumed that if fifth graders could learn to use the strategy, so could anyone who was at that chronological mental age or older.

The nature of the instructional program

The ACT instructional materials used to teach the strategy to our treatment group were programmed. By this we mean that a teacher could pick these instructional materials up, read the directions, and present the instruction to their classroom of children with no prior knowledge. That's correct: with NO prior knowledge whatsoever of their instructional content. The teacher needed only be skilled in coordinating the use of an audiotape player and a film projector and in directing children to work in individual workbooks. The teacher would also at times be involved in correcting check tests and worksheets using a key.

The instructional materials consisted of 32 lessons of about 40 minutes each. Every lesson was paced by an audiotape that provided the directions for the lessons to the children. The children were required to listen to the audiotapes, view the filmstrips, make entries in their workbooks, or journals, as we called them, take check tests, and engage in a range of activities as directed by the audiotape. One example of this kind of activity was a ring-toss game, where they were led to keep a record of their achievement while playing the game.

These instructional materials were subsequently published by McGraw-Hill[2] and are currently out of print. However, a copy of this instructional is available for inspection. Every word, every filmstrip, and every workbook can be viewed and examined today. There are also audio scripts for the lessons in which every word spoken can be heard. Hence, this treatment can be replicated in every detail. There is no mystery here.

Also, please note that the testing of this treatment was two steps away from the instructional developers as it was put in the field by individuals who were not involved in its creation. The teachers who used the materials did not have any contact with or knowledge of the material developers or evaluators. This was a truly "hands-off" test of the efficacy of the materials and of the instructional content. Finally, the materials and their content were tested in the real world of schools with real teachers and real children. This really was a "field test."

Study sample

Students from three fifth-grade classes in each of 33 schools in the Philadelphia metropolitan area participated in the field test. In each school one fifth-grade class received ACT, a second class received Curriculum X (a comparison package), and a third class received no special program, referred to as the Uninstructed Control. Classes within each school were randomly assigned to the three groups.

The comparison program, Curriculum X, was selected from published affective curriculum materials appropriate for use with fifth- and sixth-grade children. Other criteria for selection were that the comparison program be reasonably priced and that it be educationally worthwhile in its own right.

Special conditions

The field test was planned largely as a "hands-off" test under optimal conditions. Therefore, certain guidelines for use of the package were specified, and the use of the package in each classroom was monitored periodically by field managers. Both the ACT Program and Curriculum X programs were accompanied by teacher's manuals to enable the teacher to conduct them without formal training. However, to achieve optimal testing conditions, orientation and training sessions were conducted with teachers in both programs. All teachers were also asked to fill out a reaction form after each lesson, and ACT teachers were further asked to tabulate student responses to selected items on lesson tests.

Time guidelines for the use of ACT and Curriculum X were suggested. Teachers were asked to devote approximately 2 to 2-1/2 class hours per week to program activities. ACT took an average total time of 32 class hours to administer. Total duration of the field test varied between 5 and 7 months, with Curriculum X generally being completed in 4 to 5 months.

The Evaluation: A Constellation of Effects and Judgments

At the end of the instructional program all the children were tested. The tests, their results, and judgments concerning the significance of the test results formed a constellation of effects and judgments that needed to be considered as a whole. They included:

- Evidence of content learning;
- Changes in belief in internal control;
- Changes in the disposition to prescribe self directed solutions;
- Behavioral changes in setting standards for personal success;
- Behavioral changes in estimating success;
- Anecdotal reports of use of the strategy in the lives of the learners;
- Structured interviews of the children and the teachers;
- Reports of the use of the strategy by the individual classes as a class group;
- An inspection of the classroom products; and
- An independent peer review.

Evaluation results

1. Content learning. We tested the ACT treatment group to see how well students learned the content of the curriculum. Did they learn the strategy? Did they learn the skills, such as how to set a medium-risk, do-able, specific goal? We administered a straight-out old-fashioned content exam. Did they know the words? Could they demonstrate the skills? Could they answer questions that illustrated cognitive understanding? In the main, the students did well. As you might expect some did better than others, but overall we were satisfied that the treatment group learned the instructional content. This fact is extremely important because if the treatment group did not learn the instructional content, all other measures would become meaningless.

2. Belief in internal control. We tested all groups with pre- and post-measures of belief in the locus of control[3] and found that the treatment group grew significantly more than the other groups in their belief, and that this difference in directional change of the ACT group is definite and unambiguous. The graph below (see Figure 6) portrays the difference in effects.

Figure 6: Group changes in belief in locus of control scores.

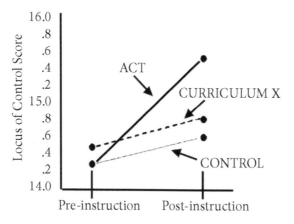

Mean scores on locus of control
shown as a function of instruction

This significant finding would alone be sufficient to justify and validate the effectiveness of teaching the Personal Achievement Strategy. With no apologies for being redundant, I invoke the research reported in Chapter 3 to point out that by inference we had significantly moved these children toward:

- Experiencing greater personal well-being;
- Displaying more motivation to innovate, complete tasks, and perform well;
- Exhibiting superior cognitive functioning;
- Being more successful in learning and academic achievement;
- Being more active and effective in social and sociopolitical behavior;
- Being more successful in work and economic endeavors;
- Engaging in healthier behavior, being healthier, and living longer;
- Being happier; and
- Taking responsibility and resisting outside influences, necessary precursors for moral behavior.

This single result, an increase in belief in internal control, compares very favorably with the results of many other internal control educational and laboratory treatment programs that have been judged to be successful,[4] but this is just the beginning of our report of the significant effects that we were able to document.

3. A measure of prescribing self-directed solutions for problems. This written test was administered to all groups pre- and post-instruction. After participating in ACT, the treatment group clearly showed a significantly greater disposition than either of the other two groups to prescribe self-directed solutions for the problems presented.

A sample question from the Summer Camp Test is provided below:[5]

Summer Camp Test: Question #12 of 14 Total Questions.

Craig: "I was getting better at horseback riding for a while, but then something happened that made me so mad I'll never go near a horse again. I got on my horse one day, and the cinch was so loose that the saddle slipped off and I fell on the ground. I'm so mad at the stupid horse for doing that to me."

As Craig's counselor, what would you do?

a. Tell him he should have learned earlier that horseback riding is too dangerous.

b. Tell him you're sorry the horse did such a mean thing to him.

c. Tell him to think about any mistakes he might have made, such as not checking to see that the cinch was tight before he got on the horse.

Note that this specific question focuses directly upon taking responsibilities for the consequences of one's actions. Other questions focus on other internal control behaviors.

Again, the results from this measure were definite and unambiguous. The following graph portrays the clear effect of the ACT (see Figure 7).

Figure 7: Group changes in the prescription of self-directed solutions.

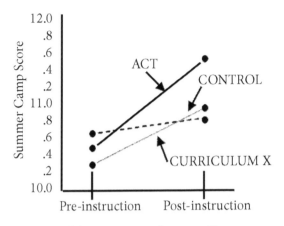

Mean scores on Summer Camp
Test shown as a function of instruction

The results of this measure taken together with the measure of belief in internal control demonstrate the impact of teaching the Personal Achievement Strategy on both the cognition and the belief systems of the children: they got it, they believed it, and they were prepared to do it. As a result of learning the strategy, these children became more self-directed and exhibited internal control!

4. Expectations for success / 5. Attainment of personally set standards for success. These two tests are measures of behavior, not simply paper and pencil-imagined situations, but those that were masked...disguised. Children were not informed about what was being measured, just encouraged to do their best in the game. They competed with each other and/or themselves and participated with enthusiasm. Each child was asked to predict her success in the game, then play the game, and then to record her success. The children did this three times for each game, a Connect the Numbers Game and a Scrambled Words Game.[6]

To give you a better understanding of these measures, I've included the directions to the Connect the Numbers Game as it was presented to the children.

Connect the Numbers Game

"In this game the numbers from 1 to 80 have been scrambled so that they are out of order. Your job is to find the number 1 and draw a line from the number 1 to the number 2. Then draw a line from number 2 to number 3, from the 3 to the number 4, and so on."

An example is presented and discussed. The children are then given the following directions:

"The first time you play the game it will be for practice. You will have 20 seconds to look at the page of numbers and then you will have 1 minute to connect as many numbers as you can starting with the number 1. After the practice game there will be 3 regular rounds of the game. Before each of these rounds you will also have 20 seconds to look at the page of numbers for that round. Then you will predict which number you will be able to reach in 1 minute and what number you would have to reach before you would say you did a good job. After each time you play the game, you will record the number you were able to reach in that round."

For each round of the game the children were asked to fill in the following questions:

a.   What number do you think you will be able to reach?

b.   What number would you have to reach before you would say you did a good job?

c.   What number did you reach?

Two different indices were measured by tests for the *expectation for success* and for the *expectation for the attainment of personal standards of success*.

5. Measuring the expectation for success. This measure records the "attainment discrepancy," or the difference between one's prediction of what score one expects to attain and what score one actually attains (the difference between a. and c. in the question above). The difference is a measure of the children's realistic judgment of their expected level of success. By this measure, the children in the ACT group were statistically more realistic than the other children in predicting the level of their performance. There was a smaller difference between a. and c. for this group.

6. Measuring personal standards for success. This measure records the "Standard Discrepancy," or the difference between one's personal standards for a good job and what one actually expects to attain (the difference between b. and c. in the question above). The differences between the ACT learner's personal standards for a good job and what s/he actually expected to gain were significantly less than either the alternate treatment group or the no treatment group. One could say that the ACT learners had more reasonable expectations for doing well or, stated another way, that they had more realistic standards for their personal success. The importance of this finding seems considerable when one infers that the internal control learners now have a greater opportunity to experience subjective success and favorable self-evaluation. These findings are one of the most important effects of teaching the Personal Achievement Strategy, particularly insofar as they illuminate the process of changes in goal-setting behavior.

In the 1960s, Dr. I. Katz developed a model of achievement based on the premise that striving for achievement is sustained by the quality of covert reinforcement that the learner administers to himself.[7] If this is true, it follows that training in internal control behavior would hinge on making these covert reinforcements more favorable. One can also increase the learner's subjective experience of success by causing the internal control learner to lower his subjective standards of success in order to reduce the discrepancy between the standard and his expected or actual performance. This, in turn, leads to an increased sense of internal control.

One example that comes to mind is that of a child learning to play a musical instrument. The child may start out with the unreasonable expectation that he is going to begin playing just like the professionals he hears on recordings. Parents and music instructors know this is a prescription for failure, so they hasten to coach the child to lower his expectations for his beginning efforts. They know that the child will become discouraged and cease to try if his initial expectations are too high. They are correct. Initial high expectations result in debilitating negative reinforcement for the beginner.

I have to say that I am ecstatic over these effects. These are *behavior changes*! These are *very significant internal control behavior changes*. These changes will make a difference in the lives of the treatment children, and are essential to beginning and maintaining the **upward spiral of achievement > internal control >**. I believe there are few, if any, behavioral changes like this in any other research effort and certainly none on this scale even today!

7. Using the strategy: Anecdotal reports. Anecdotal reports alone should not be considered as validation of a treatment, but without them the effects of the instructional treatment might be suspect. Furthermore, the content of the anecdotes can illuminate the meaning and significance of the effects of the treatment in real life examples that help us better understand its effects. Finally, anecdotal reports in combination with other kinds of data can powerfully confirm the effects of an instructional treatment.[8]

We invested in collecting a considerable volume of anecdotal reports from children, teachers, and parents. We summarized, analyzed, and published many of these as a part of our evaluation report[9] (which again can be accessed at teachinternalcontrol. com). The following anecdotes and summaries are largely in the voice and words of staff member Peter Beckingham:

What follows is a summary and some examples of how the children used the strategy and their comments about their experience.

Comments about the ACT program reflect major effects in two areas: planning and self-awareness. This may be a function of where the children were in the progression of the instruction when we began to collect these anecdotes. First, children talked most consistently about the planning concepts, which seemed to be something that was, if not new to them, at least meaningful to them for the first time. Although not all children were writing lists of tasks, most were at least applying forethought to their activities.

Second, the children talked about their strengths and, in some cases, their weaknesses, and what they could do to work on them. Most of the children seemed more self-directed after participating in the treatment program, and in many cases were more conscious of this sense of self-agency.

The following anecdotes are just a small sample of those we collected. As you read them, ask yourself, "Do these notes illuminate, illustrate, and confirm the effects of teaching the Personal Achievement Strategy?" All the names of participating children have been changed.

Beckingham goes on to provide examples, as below:

The Children Speak

Eric, who is very keen on diving, said he had used the Achievement Worksheets to set goals for this activity. He showed me his current worksheet on which he had written the goal, "To achieve a double somersault in two weeks." He reported he had told the instructor who was working with him about his goal. Eric said that he felt that using the Achievement Strategy concepts had helped him. The biggest change he noticed was in the way he had learned to focus on one specific thing at a time and to aim for that.

Linda said she liked the Strength Survey because she found out more about herself. She had not realized before how many strengths she had in the area of physical activities. Linda reported using the strategy out of school: she had set a goal to get into the Philadelphia Tennis Gold Cup competition. By using the planning concept, she set aside time for practice. As a striving method she pictured herself taking part in the competition. She feels the strategy is definitely helping her, and at the same time thought the lessons were fun.

Joanne told me about her experience of having to help at home when her mother was sick, and how she planned what tasks she had to do. From the way she spoke, I sensed that the planning had helped her to feel in control of the situation. She also said that because of the strategy she felt capable of doing more things.

Mark related that now he did more planning in his head. He said that he felt more aware of his strengths, and that knowing them made him feel good. He then told me about a goal he had to set to become first trumpet in the junior band. When I asked him if he had used a striving method, he said that he had pictured himself as the first trumpet player. He was smiling as he said this, and I had the impression that here was a boy who thought in terms of success and who had found the strategy useful.

Ellen told me she had set a goal to swim 50 laps in the club pool. She didn't make it, but said as a result she had learned not to set too high a goal in the future. She also told me about a goal she had set to make a foreign doll. She recounted how she planned for it and how very proud she felt when finished. She gave it to her dad for a birthday present. "He said it was beautiful," she added with a grin. This success gave her further ideas for sewing activities, and she next set a goal to make a pillow for her mother's anniversary.

Do these anecdotes help you better understand the impact that teaching the Personal Achievement Strategy has on the lives of children?

. . .

Now let's review a summary of the teachers' comments and a report of two teachers' experiences. Remember, there were 33 teachers who used the instructional materials. Other interviews are available in our evaluation report.[10]

Interestingly, the same dominant effects emerged from the teachers' point of view after teaching the Personal Achievement

Strategy as emerged from the children's: increased self-awareness and the use of the concept of planning. In addition, the teachers reported that the children were more organized, more autonomous (both individually and as a class), more accepting of one another, and more cooperative. Wow! What more could anyone ask?

The Teachers Speak

Russell Scaramastra reported an instance in which the Achieve Competence Training helped children to work together more effectively. One of his reading groups was to put on a play for the class. Some of the group were in the ACT class, while others were not. At first the children bickered and argued about how the play should be put on. Finally, a boy who had been a group leader in the ACT class suggested that they choose a group leader to get things written down. The others agreed, and the group began to plan for the play. It was obvious, Mr. Scaramastra said, that the initiative was taken by the children who were in the Personal Achievement Strategy training program.

After his class started working with ACT, Mr. Scaramastra reported noticing a general improvement. There was less chaos and the children seemed more open. They became used to sharing and exchanging information. These changes, he felt, were directly attributable to the group-sharing behavior they practiced in the Achievement Strategy lessons. He also added that the youngsters seemed more willing to hear other points of view.

Mr. Scaramastra also found that his class's project work was of a much better quality. This change he also attributed to the Personal Achievement Strategy because he had not directly talked about or practiced behaviors or strategies for improving project work. "The strategy gives you a basis to spring from," he explained. He told of one boy who was having trouble getting started with a social studies project. He met with the boy, referred to the strategy, and suggested some striving steps. Apparently it worked because after that the boy did begin his project.

Achievement Worksheets are used generally by the children for projects in class, but Mr. Scaramastra reported that they proved especially helpful with one of his slower students. First he talked with the boy and helped him set a goal. Then he showed him how to plan for it using the worksheet. Later the boy changed some of the tasks and re-planned, and finally he achieved his goal.

This is a short statement from another teacher, Carol-Lynne Wiley. Ms. Wiley told me that she had received several unsolicited comments about her ACT class. A substitute teacher had said that the class seemed to be much more organized and independent than the other one (control class) she had taught. The librarian had also mentioned that the children in the in the ACT class seemed to be more independent and better able to work by themselves in the library.

Ms. Wiley felt these characteristics could be attributed to behaviors the children learned from the Achievement Competence Training, ACT.

Again, I believe these anecdotes make up just one of the points in the constellation of evidence further validating the effectiveness of teaching the Personal Achievement Strategy. With that in mind, we will now look at another example of supporting evidence.

. . .

8. Structured interviews. Structured interviews are another way of studying the effects of a treatment and are, again, much more significant and confirming when considered in combination with other measurements.[11] "Structured interviews" incorporate a list of specific questions created for the purposes of obtaining answers from randomly selected children and teachers. Because one of the purposes of this evaluation was to collect information to help us revise the instructional materials and make them more effective before publication, most of these questions focused on the instructional materials and their effectiveness. Some of the questions, however, did focus on the effects of the overall instructional program. These results are published and are also available for your review online.

The following are several children's answers to one of the questions asked in the structured interview.

The Question: Have you used the Personal Achievement Strategy outside of school?

Student #1: Yes. Planning—we had a party for my sister and I wrote it down on paper—what to do in order. Re-planning—if somebody didn't have what they needed for the party we had to re-plan and give it to somebody else to do.

Student #2: Yes, painting the house. First I got the paint, put the cloth down, got a ladder and brushes andstarted painting. I'm using one now—saving money to get a mini-bike.

Student #3: Yes, a little to play football.

Student #4: Yes.

Student #5: No.

Student # 6: Yes. We were going to make a fort and we didn't know if we could do it. We planned how to do it.

Student # 7: Yeah. For almost three years my dad said he was gonna take us ice fishing but he never did it, so I got one of those Achievement Worksheets and filled it out and we did it.

Student # 8: Yes. [Named the six steps.] Used them in acrobatics, swimming. This taught me to help my Mom around the house—clean up and pick up clothes. In acrobatics, I worked hard to do handstands for the gym program.

Student #9: I didn't want to use them. Sometimes when I have a problem, I listen to music, but I did that all along.

Student #10: Yes, for Study Self I asked myself if I should play with this girl—why should I and why shouldn't I?

Hmmm…well, welcome to the world of real data. I am not sure we might expect when randomly selecting 10 children from a pool of approximately 900, but in this case we got two negatives and eight positives. Do these children's answers help you better understand the kind of impact that teaching the Personal Achievement Strategy can have on the lives of children? I believe they do.

Here are some of the teachers' answers to one of the questions in their structured interviews.

The question: Have you seen any benefits to the class or to individuals which you would attribute to teaching the Personal Achievement Strategy?

Teacher #1: [This teacher simply offered the following list] Discussion skills; decision-making skills; listening skills; taking turns; some are setting goals; all have learned to interact better; group cohesion has developed; food for beginning teacher; teacher can be more human.

Teacher #2: No question about this. This class has never been cohesive. This program has given them this. They work better in committees and in planning. One boy was new and of less ability. He was not accepted at first. As the program developed he emerged as a more interesting person and was accepted by the group. Leaders emerged and they took their roles in good spirit.

Teacher #3: More to individuals than to class as a whole. Many better students are planning units in social studies and science better, budgeting time, et cetera. Some have mentioned tasks outside of school. They can use worksheets for these.

Teacher #4: They are using the terms, strategies, et cetera. They are working together better than ever before.

Teacher #5: I have seen individuals who are setting goals, making lists, and planning. It hasn't helped lower-achieving students. They haven't grasped concepts. They haven't been able to set goals. Most of the top students gained. Some of these felt bored listening to the tapes.

Teacher #6: One child came in and said, "You know, I really finished that belt." Class meetings are better run. Class is beginning to learn how to work together. In election of student council they used some of the strategy in evaluating the candidates.

Teacher #7: No.

Teacher #8: Individually it helped many. The planning was valuable. They applied this to their social studies.

Teacher # 9: Student who lacked self-confidence was helped the most. Setting goals was a constant reminder. It had to come from within them. There was a carryover in other areas. Setting goals has become a part of everyday routine.

Teacher #10: Definitely some are evaluating themselves pretty well. What they can say they think they'll get right and strive for it. This can be used for every area of study. Putting time limits on themselves; also, getting into groups.

Teacher #11: Much more than I realized would be. Kids who were totally disorganized now can plan. One kid lies in bed in the morning and plans his day. A lot has rubbed off on me.

In my estimation, answers further validate the effectiveness of teaching the Personal Achievement Strategy.

9. Classroom Projects. Another point in our constellation of instructional effects is comprised of classroom observations made as the children worked on the final unit of the instructional program. In this unit the children were called upon to work together to employ the strategy to carry out a class project.

These class projects were all successful to one degree or another. Teachers, parents and the children themselves were pleased with the results. Again, these reports are published for your review online. Here are two quoted summarized examples.

Lower Salford School; Teacher: Dorothy J. Krapf

Earlier, this class had expressed disinterest in the ACT program. Some of the children had set only perfunctory goals, not seeing the relevance of the strategy. They did set a class goal, however: "To have a talent show for charity in three weeks."

During the course of the group project the children changed their attitudes. They became very much motivated by what they were doing. Several committees were set up to accomplish the many tasks the class had outlined. One committee, for example, auditioned all the children who applied to be in the show. Ms. Krapf told me that the class was taking the goal very seriously and really working at it with enthusiasm.

The show was a great success and merited the amount of work put into it. There were 23 acts presented before several hundred students, parents, and friends. A voluntary donation of 10 cents was requested, and the money was given to the Cancer Society. The local newspaper printed a story and a picture of the show."

Ms. Krapf told me that the children felt really great about themselves. She also reported that the parents and the principal were very pleased with both the performances and with the whole idea of the event being planned and run by the children. The principal wrote a letter to the class, congratulating the children on their efforts, which also added to their self-esteem.

Woodlyn School; Teacher: Albert Ramos

The class goal was, "To hold pet show on Wednesday afternoon, April 18 from 1:15 to 2:15." [Not only was this goal achieved, but Mr. Ramos reported that the event was generally considered to be a "howling success."] There were fourteen dogs, five cats, seven mice, one guinea pig, and one snake. Each person who brought a pet received a framed certificate and a ribbon. Each animal was declared a winner in some category.

The youngsters decided on the categories, designed the certificates, colored them, drew the ribbon medallions, made the placards, decided the winners for each category, originated other categories where necessary, and controlled their animals well.

The high degree of the involvement and motivation that was common to many of the class goals is evident in this teacher's report.

I believe that the reports of these class projects clearly demonstrate the effectiveness of teaching our strategy. The children were able to effectively use the strategy to carry out their projects in an autonomous and effective manner. They took control and did their thing. They succeeded in effectively acting on their environment and in making a difference about things they cared about and in which they were interested. That is internal control at its best!

10. Inspection of learner products. During the course of the instructional program the children were required to produce "products" as a part of the required activities. These products included lists of strengths, lists of past achievement, lists of goal ideas (set by the children as specific and medium risk), and Achievement Worksheets. As a part of our evaluation we collected these products and examined them. Were the children able to do the work? Did the quality and content of the products reflect our objectives?

For the most part, our investigation of the large volume of products collected indicated that the children were doing the work correctly. There is no way that we can share all these instructional products in this context, but you will note that we have already offered examples of these products to illustrate previous points. We will continue to utilize these examples in the following pages.

In order to make the point that these tools can be significant in helping to evaluate the effectiveness of this instructional program, I offer an example of a key tool, an Achievement Worksheet. I do this for two reasons: first, the Achievement Worksheets are mentioned several times in the preceding anecdotes by teachers and students, who reported using them both in school and out of school and often outside the purview of the instructional materials. They were perceived as useful and they seemed to "catch on." Second, the Achievement Worksheets are a snapshot of the strategy in action. A filled-out Achievement Worksheet is a specific portrayal of the individual's belief in internal control in action. The child is taking control of her life and acting to accomplish or attain something that she has consciously decided she wants to do. This is internal control in a nutshell—or, in these two cases, in two pages. Take a look (see Figure 8).

Figure 8: Evaluation of the Personal Achievement Strategy instruction's Total Constellation of Effects.

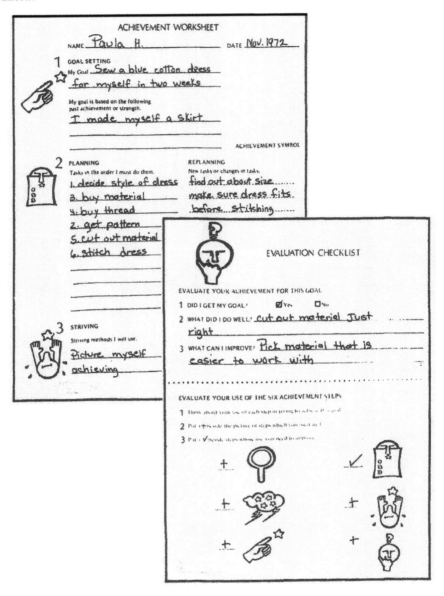

Let's take a moment to summarize the points of evidence in what I am calling a "constellation of evidence," or "constellation of effects and judgments" (see Figure 9).

Figure 9: Constellation of Effects and Judgments.

As a result of the ACT instructional program, the children:

- Learned the concepts and the skills of the strategy and could demonstrate their use;
- Exhibited a significant positive change in belief in internal control;
- Were more likely to prescribe self-directed solutions to problems;
- Made more realistic predictions of their performance; and
- Set more realistic standards for their successful performance.

Furthermore:

- Anecdotal reports documented the use of the strategy in the lives of the children outside of the classroom.
- Structured interviews of the children and the teachers documented use of the strategy by the children in and out of school.
- Reports of the use of the strategy by the classes during their class projects documented effective use of the strategy.
- An inspection of the products produced by the learners during the instructional program documented effective use of the strategy.

One additional note: One of the scientific conditions necessary for claiming that a hypothesis is supportable is that the results, and therefore the treatment, can be replicated. This treatment, the ACT program, can be replicated down to the timed instructional directions. The program exists in three, 3" x 9.5" x 13" boxes. With a reasonable amount of preparation it can be functioning in a classroom within months.

Given the above information, I find that this constellation of evaluative evidence unequivocally and overwhelming supports the hypotheses that *teaching the Personal Achievement Strategy results in greater internality.*

But one issue remains. Just because we obtained some movement in the direction of internality, does that mean this movement is meaningful? Is it significant in a practical sense? Will it make a practical, real-life difference in children's lives? Or is it just an interesting mathematical artifact?

As an example, if one person were to score three points higher on an intelligence test than a second person and this difference were statistically significant, we would still need to ask, "Is this difference *practically* significant?" That is, does this statistically significant difference make any practical difference in the real-life behavior of these two people?

I, of course, have a clear and very strong opinion that our evaluation results show that teaching the Personal Achievement Strategy was and is practically significant. But it is also obvious that I am biased.

Frankly, even at the time of this field study I didn't trust my own opinion alone—nor should I have. Therefore, in order to deal with this judgment issue, we hired an independent evaluator who had no connection to our institution, staff, or project, but who was knowledgeable, published, and recognized in this and related areas of research to help us.

When Richard Teevan, Ph.D., a professionally recognized researcher and writer and, at the time of this evaluation, Chairman of the Psychology Department of SUNY, Albany, studied our evaluation data in detail he made the following statement:

> There is no statistical way to determine whether or not a given difference is practically significant. In order to get an answer to this crucial question, I went over all of the comments of the teachers, the comments of the students, and the comments of the observers. I especially looked for comments that suggested that the children were more self-initiating, felt better about themselves, were able to work better, etc. In view of these comments and the statistical findings, it is my opinion that the results are practically as well as statistically significant.

. . .

The following chapters focus upon the nitty-gritty of teaching the Personal Achievement Strategy.

Chapter 5

Teach the Personal Achievement Strategy: The Specifics

Teaching the Personal Achievement Strategy is fun and satisfying, so get ready for an exciting time. Learners really get involved. Morale goes up. And why not? When learners start by identifying past achievements and strengths and sharing their past achievements with others, they feel great. When they build on these same achievements and strengths to take control of their lives step by step, they become excited by the possibility, the growing belief that they can successfully achieve goals that are meaningful to them. Enthusiasm builds and continues as the participants learn to use the steps of the Personal Achievement Strategy. Smiles abound.

The Central Hypothesis

Before we begin discussing the details of teaching the Personal Achievement Strategy, let's review. As you know by now, it is our hypothesis that we can effectively teach internal locus of control by teaching the Personal Achievement Strategy. Let's be confident in why we believe this is so. This hypothesis is supported by the following points:

1. The strategy has logical and face validity. If you want to influence the course of your life, setting personal goals and striving to achieve these same goals is a way to do it. It is a viable answer to the question, "What should I do to exercise internal control of my life?"

2. Research documents that achievement experience predictably results in an increase in belief in internal locus of control (as reported in Chapter 1). Teaching the strategy increases the achievement experiences of the learner, which then in turn predictably increases belief in internal locus of control.

3. The strategy's viability is supported by studies showing that several of its individual components such as goal setting, task listing, and evaluation of personal actions, predictably increases belief in internal locus of control.

4. The claim that teaching and using the strategy increases belief in internal locus of control and internal control-like behavior is strongly supported by the field evaluation study reported in the last chapter (Chapter 4).

5. Individuals consistently report a greater sense of internal control as a result of using the strategy. When individuals set personal goals and experience success in achieving these goals, they see that they are significantly influencing the course of their lives.

Now that we are secure in our understanding of why we are teaching the Personal Achievement Strategy, let's explore ideas about how to teach it.

Teaching the Personal Achievement Strategy

In order to help you become an effective and knowledgeable teacher of the Personal Achievement Strategy I offer the following:

1. Instructional behavioral objectives that define the desired outcomes of the instructional program;
2. Three steps to help you prepare to teach the strategy;
3. A description of four formats that you might use to teach the strategy;
4. A check list of principles, procedures, and activities that can be helpful in your teaching; and
5. A call to learn to personally use the strategy in order to empower yourself as a teacher.

Instructional objectives

The list of instructional objectives listed below specify the desired outcomes of an instructional program designed to teach the Personal Achievement Strategy. These objectives state what your learners *should* be able to do at the end of your instruction. Teach these behaviors and you will teach learners to think and act as Internals.

With respect to the Personal Achievement Strategy, learners will be able upon request to:

1. Name the strategy steps in order;
2. Give a hypothetical example of how they might use the strategy or how they have used the strategy in their lives;
3. Report in modest detail the past use of the strategy to achieve one or more personal goals; and
4. Name three or more reasons for learning to use the strategy from the list of desirable behaviors correlating with internal locus of control (listed in

chapter 2), such as to increase a sense of well-being, to improve cognitive functioning, to increase school success, or to increase happiness.

With respect to the individual strategy steps, learners will be able upon request to:

1. List personal past achievements;
2. List personal strengths;
3. List personal areas of interest;
4. State why it is valuable to be knowledgeable about past achievements, strengths, and interests;
5. Generate goal ideas from their lists of past achievements, strengths, and interests;
6. Formulate goal ideas that are doable and short term;
7. Formulate goal ideas that are specific in time, kind, and number;
8. Formulate goal ideas that are medium risk;
9. Report setting personal goals and name one or more goals that they are currently striving to achieve;
10. Plan, name, and order the tasks required to be completed in order to achieve a specific goal they have set;
11. Question and seek information about a plan for a personal goal and to re-plan when given new information;
12. Strive; that is, to proceed to work toward completing the planned tasks for the achievement of their goal;
13. Describe how they might use striving techniques, including but not limited to remembering past achievements, picturing success, and finding inspiration in the attributes of heroes, competition with others, competition with self, and competition with standards of excellence;

14. Evaluate the results of their efforts to decide if they have achieved the goal they set;

15. Evaluate their performance to decide what went well, what could be improved, and how it could be improved;

16. Evaluate their use of the personal achievement strategy and report how they could improve their use of the strategy; and

17. Utilize the strategy steps as a unified whole to achieve personal goals in three or more domains.

That's it. That's all there is. An experienced teacher, parent, or supervisor can utilize these instructional behavioral objectives to created an instructional program tailored to their situation and to their learners. Teach these behaviors and your learners will be empowered; they will *be* "Internals."

But let's take another moment to be clear about what I mean when I say "teach":

1. Your learners will be able to verbally describe the above concepts and ideas.

2. Your learners will be able to perform the above skills and procedures upon request.

3. Your learners will display these attitudes and engage in these behaviors in their life situations apart from the instructional situation.

Allow me to offer an analogy. All health-care workers are taught Universal Precaution Procedures.[1] One of these procedures consists of the importance of and the method for effective hand-washing. Learners in this situation have to be able to describe the reasons and the procedures of hand-washing in paper and pencil exams and they have to demonstrate the procedure in live situations. But the real test is whether these learners appropriately use these procedures when they are not aware they are being observed. If they don't, the teachers of this procedure have failed to "teach" this behavior. If the learners do wash their hands at times when they believe they are not being observed, then the teacher will have been successful in teaching this procedure.

So it is with the Personal Achievement Strategy. If our learners do not use the strategy in their lives when they are not being observed then we have failed. This is the reason that I am so ecstatic about the findings of the evaluation reported in the last chapter, where the learners exhibited the target behaviors in disguised testing situations and where life use of internal behaviors was further supported by anecdotes of the teachers, parents, and the learners themselves. The strategy was being used by the learners in situations when they were not aware they were being observed! This is the most desirable of all educational objectives: real life use. So this is what I mean when I say that "teaching" the information implies that learners actually use the Personal Achievement Strategy in their lives.

Preparing to Teach

Before you begin to teach the Personal Achievement Strategy, it is useful to engage in some preparatory thinking. There are three things you can do that will make your teaching easier and more effective.

1. Select Domains: First, you need to select the domain(s) in which you intend to have the learners practice employing the Personal Achievement Strategy steps. For example, you might decide upon a very wide-angle focus, such as "all life," where anything of interest to the learner will be acceptable as a goal. Or you may limit the domain(s) in which you want the learners to practice the strategy steps. This was my approach in the instructional program reported in Chapter 5. In that program I asked the learners to set goals in any one of five domains that I thought would be appropriate and of interest to fifth-grade learners. These domains were crafts, interpersonal relations, school subjects, art, and athletics. You may want your learners to focus even more sharply. One example of a sharper focus might be a teacher working with learners to create science projects for a science fair. Another example might be a parent working with his child to set goals to improve school grades. Once you have selected the domain(s) on which you intend to focus it's time to prepare to introduce your instructional program.

2. Develop Goal Ideas: As a first step in introducing your domain of focus you need to develop goal ideas that will interest and attract your learners; that is, some goals that you imagine your learners would really like to achieve. Your initial objective is to get the learners to want to achieve…to *do* something. You need to prime the pump by being able to suggest possible goals that excite and inspire. For example, if you are a sales manger you might want to suggest that people like your learners can improve their sales effectiveness and income by learning and applying proven sales techniques. You want to communicate that they can become sales stars. You might have some top salesmen visit and provide testimony and pep talks. You might have the learners make a list of things they would do if they were to increase their income by fifty percent. Project hope, create excitement, and put stars in the eyes of your learners.

As another example, if you are the teacher working with your learners to plan and create science projects, you will want to suggest exciting projects that your learners can create. You can give examples of past winning projects and recount the experience of the students who created them. Have your learners dream of conducting a study that is widely recognized. Think through how you will motivate your learners to want to do something, to achieve their goal, and have a collection of ideas and anecdotes that you can draw on to excite them.

3. Create a learner-oriented learning situation: Once you have inspired your learners to want to achieve in the domain which you have selected, you should introduce the Personal Achievement Strategy as a tool that will enable them to achieve their goals. You want your learners to be motivated to learn to use the strategy in order to enable them to achieve their personally identified goals. This will allow you to act in the role of coach and counselor, helper and assistant. The learners will be the principle doers, the actors, the agents. They will be the drivers. This puts you in the position of saying, "If you set specific goals you are better able to achieve your selected goal. So, let's work on goal-setting and also striving techniques so you'll be more successful in achieving your goal."

In this way, a "learner–oriented" learning situation is created. The purpose of learning the strategy becomes that of helping the learners to achieve their goals. This contrasts with a "teacher–oriented" learning situation, where the learners are learning to use the strategy because the teacher says so and where the learning objective is that of the teacher. In this case s/he is the actor, the agent, the driver…s/he is exerting power, even threats, to make the learners learn. Good luck! You do not want to be in this role. This is a contradiction of Internality. We want to avoid being in the position of requiring our learners to become Externals in order to learn to become Internals. When you are learner-oriented you work together with your learners, shoulder to shoulder, to help them learn to employ the Personal Achievement Strategy to achieve their goals. As the agents and their own deciders, they, the learners, assume responsibility for learning for their own purposes. With a learner orientation approach you are setting the stage for introducing a successful instructional program.

Personal Achievement Strategy: Teaching Formats

In this section I present four different formats for teaching your internal control program. You might choose any of them as a guide for the creation of your own curriculum:

- The workshop format
- The school curriculum format
- The inductive format
- The employer format

I'll describe and discuss each one.

1. The workshop format. The objective of the workshop format is to *teach* the use of the Personal Achievement Strategy. Participants receive instruction about how to use each step of the strategy. After the instruction concerning the use of a given strategy step, the participants are asked to use the step within the context of their current life. The participants actually list their past achievements, develop goal ideas, and proceed through each of the strategy steps as a part of their learning experience. They further learn the strategy by applying the strategy to their current life activities. Participants light up during these activities and become engaged and enthusiastic. IT REALLY WORKS!

This format operates like many workshops. The participants form groups of eight to ten with as many groups as you and your staff can handle. You provide a brief informational overview, review group procedures, and start presenting the steps. After you present each step with some illustrations and activities, you ask the participants to apply the strategy step to their lives. Finally, the participants share their experiences with the members of their group and discuss their experiences as they proceed.

For example, you may be introducing the concept of "medium risk." In this case, you might employ a ring-toss game as an activity to engage the learners and to illustrate risk in goal setting. Ring toss is a game very much like quoits or horseshoes, where participants predict their performance and then strive to throw the rope rings on or by the target pole. As the learners participate, they reveal and portray a range of risk taking. This is fun, engaging, and very revealing. The participants then discuss their experiences and proceed to set their own goal at a medium risk level.

As an example of a brief and simple workshop, I developed a 45-minute session for presentation at evening PTA meetings in which I promoted parental understanding and acceptance for teaching the Personal Achievement Strategy in their school. When I led this workshop, I immediately put parents into groups and guided them in applying the strategy to their current everyday lives. The parents responded enthusiastically. When these parents talked with other parents, even those they hardly knew, they became interested and understanding users of the strategy. Several times over the ensuing years people came up to me in public places to tell me that they made and followed through on significant decisions as a result of those single evening meetings. Hard to believe, but true! One woman, an acquaintance, became a very successful realtor and has repeatedly thanked me through the years.

Who me? Wow. Terrific!

A creditable and effective workshop can be conducted within 2-1/2 hours or expanded to 3 or more hours (not counting break time). The difference depends on the amount of time you devote to developing plans for implementation of the strategy in a specific domain or situation. For example, you may be working with a school faculty and plan to have the teachers work together to develop suggestions for school-wide applications of the strategy.

Again, activities are important. We want the participants to have *experiences*, not just listen and talk. For ideas for how to design and pace a workshop, I refer you to the next format, which provides a much more extensive and detailed outline for instruction. Review this design and adapt the activities for your workshop as you wish.

3. The school curriculum format. This is a direct classroom instructional approach where there is a specific time set aside for teaching the Personal Achievement Strategy. In order to make suggestions on how to teach the strategy in a direct instructional mode, I offer an outline of the curriculum in the Achievement Competence Training (ACT) program that was evaluated and discussed in the last chapter. The ACT curriculum provides an organizational structure for thinking about teaching the strategy. You can use this curriculum design to organize your own instructional efforts. Further, this curriculum describes instructional activities and content that you will find extremely useful when teaching the strategy. (see Figure 10).

Figure 10: The Six Achievement Steps.

	1 Study Self	2 Get Goal Ideas	3 Set a Goal	4 Plan	5 Strive	6 Evaluate
	PART 1	PART 2	PART 3	PART 4	PART 5	PART 6
UNIT I	Learn to define achievement	Draw self achieving	Learn about ACT	Learn to work in a group	Set goals and strive in a game	Learn the six achievement steps
UNIT II	Name past achievements	Get goal ideas from past achievements	Make goal specific	Name and order tasks	Use envisioning, achievement, and heroes	Decide how well you did
UNIT III	Name personal strengths	Get goal ideas from strengths	Make goal medium risk	Replan when faced with problems	Use competition	Evaluate progress with ACT
UNIT IV	Name group strengths	Get goal ideas for your group	Select a group goal	Plan tasks for group	Strive for your goal	Evaluate group achievement

Note that a total of 26 cells are arrayed in four rows, representing the four units. The rows have several lessons. The first row is labeled Unit I and is concerned with introducing the learners to the instructional program and preparing them to learn to use the strategy. The next two rows, labeled Units II and III, lead the learners through two complete uses of the strategy. The fourth and last row, labeled Unit IV, leads the class as a group through the use of the strategy to create a class project. In all, the learners use the strategy three different times, twice as individuals and once as a group member. Each time the learners proceed through the use of the strategy they are taught to use the strategy more effectively.

Learning objectives are stated for each of the cells. After three uses of the strategy the learners learn to use the strategy. This experience influences learner's belief and their behavior. This is the curriculum which we used to successfully teach the

Personal Achievement Strategy in the research study described in the last chapter. Adapt it for your own learners and your own situation.

For your use, I describe the content of each cell, including subject content, activities, and supporting theory in greater detail in Chapter 7. If you plan to develop a classroom-based instructional program, I urge you to read this chapter carefully and utilize it as a resource as you proceed to build your own program as it is rich with activity ideas. If you would like even more detailed information and many more examples, I suggest that you purchase the *ACT Teacher's Manual: Achievement Training Competence* and the *ACT Student Journal: Achievement Competence Training Journal,*[2] available at teachinternalcontrol. com.

4. The inductive format. This format for teaching internal control takes an inductive, non-classroom approach, weaving the steps of the Personal Achievement Strategy into the primary activity of the specific activity in which the learners are participating. Examples include a parent, who might introduce the ideas with his/her child through planning a vacation trip together; a teacher, who might work with a class of children to set individual learning goals in mathematics or engage the children in evaluating their work on a class project; a health-care worker, who might plan with a diabetic client to establish a diet and discuss striving techniques to help the client stay on his diet; or an office manager, who might institute production planning and goal-setting meetings and ask employees to maintain to-do lists. In these cases, the Personal Achievement Strategy is introduced piecemeal, skill by skill, behavior by behavior. The situations and needs that occur in the course of the activity provide the opportunities for teaching the strategy steps and the internal control behaviors. Each step and behavior is taught as it can be employed within the purview of the immediate activity.

It may be that teaching the Personal Achievement Strategy in an inductive manner is the most effective and powerful way to teach internality. When you and your learners apply the strategy in real-life situations you get immediate feedback for your efforts; you see great things happen. Your behavior is confirmed and reinforced. You are teaching learners to use the strategy in their everyday lives.

4. The employer format. The employer format is a specific extension of the inductive teaching format. Again, you introduce the skills and ideas of the Personal Achievement Strategy as you conduct the operation of the enterprise or business in which you are engaged. But keep in mind in one very important difference. Businesses are concerned with business objectives. They are engaged in making money. They are NOT in the business of personal development, or of teaching internality.

Therefore, it is particularly important to be clear about why you would want to teach internal attitudes and behavior to employees. What makes the effort worth the time and expense? Why not just tell employees what you want them to do and hold them accountable? Isn't that is what many organizations do?

Well, because…because there is a valuable payoff to the employer for encouraging internality. Research shows that employees who exhibit internal control are better employees in the sense that they have higher levels of job commitment, job satisfaction, job performance, and leadership initiative, and also experience lower incidences of burnout, psychological strain, and role ambguity.[3] We can infer from this information that teaching internality can significantly contribute to the efficiency and effectiveness of the enterprise involved. For example, the sales manager who actively engages his sales people in setting sales and who participates in making their goals doable, specific, and medium risk will obtain commitment and buy-in from his sales force. As their motivation and determination heightens, these individuals will be more fully committed to meeting the sales goals that have been set and will feel responsible for doing so. The shipping dock supervisor who engages his laborers in a brief morning discussion about the day's objectives and schedules the tasks in consultation with the workers will see more effective and efficient execution of the work that is undertaken because he will have shared some of the planning with his workers.

When you treat your employees as agents with minds and wills not only will the morale of your employees be higher, but predictably you will have a more effective and efficient operation.

A check list of principles, procedures, and activities useful for teaching the Personal Achievement Strategy

It's always helpful to have some ideas in our back pocket for those times when we may not be feeling so inspired. That's why I want to offer a check list of concepts, suggested practices, and activities that you can pull out whenever you need them.

This check list is presented in Chapter 8 of this book because I felt that presenting this check list at this point in this book would detract from the flow of our discussion. Read through Chapter 8 as you have time. It will be especially helpful when you begin your teaching activities. You might want to make a copy of this list and review it every once in a while just for the purpose of renewing your focus and stimulating your interest and commitment in teaching Internality.

Summary

Learning to use the strategy empowers you, as a person and as a teacher.

The single most valuable thing you can do to prepare yourself to teach internal control via the Personal Achievement Strategy is to learn to use the strategy in your own life. We all know that we learn through experience, and this strategy is no different. But don't just focus on understanding the strategy in an objective, cognitive sense. Work with it. Use it in your life. Start journaling about your experiences. Take the time from your daily grind to thoughtfully write out your current life goals. Those of us who do feel the effects of the strategy very quickly. We feel more in control; we reduce and harness our anxiety. This empowers us as individuals.

Learning to use the strategy also empowers you as a teacher. The experiences you will have using the strategy will help you explain and illustrate the skill set the strategy teaches. You will see more and more possibilities for applications. You will be better able to identify and empathize with your learners. But most of all you will develop a belief and a conviction in the efficacy and power of the strategy. This conviction will shine through your presentation and energize your teaching behavior. This energy will be directly communicated to your learners.

Now you are exciting; you have emotional impact. Empowered, you are better able to empower others.

Chapter 6

Suggestions for Applying the Personal Achievement Strategy

In this chapter we will consider some possible applications of the Personal Achievement Strategy. We call these applications "sketches" because they are not meant to be complete detailed plans. In the case of our college curriculum, the ideas for teaching internal control have been in use for more than 40 years. In other cases the sketches are just ideas, proposals, and suggestions. My principle purpose is to spark your imagination. I have included sketches on the following topics:

1. Parenting
2. Addiction rehabilitation
3. Life skills for the mentally and emotional impaired
4. College-student curriculum (design currently in use at Juniata College in Huntingdon, Pennsylvania)

5. Narrowing the black-white achievement gap
   (an ongoing opportunity for research)
6. Volunteer groups, marriages, and corporations
   (in the form of a process guide)
7. School organization (for fostering internal
   control and more effective education practices)

We will now look at each one of these areas in turn.

1. Parenting. Do you want your child to:

- Experience positive personal well-being?
- Be motivated to innovate, complete tasks, and perform well?
- Exhibit effective cognitive functioning?
- Be successful in learning and academic achievement?
- Exhibit desirable social and sociopolitical behavior?
- Be successful in work and economic activities?
- Be healthy?
- Be happy?
- Take responsibility and resist outside influences?

If your answer is "yes" to the above questions, then you need to think about the evidence that we have presented in this book indicating that *teaching internal locus of control is the most significant thing you can do to assure that your child will experience and exhibit these personal qualities. Further, since research indicates that* the family is far and away the most powerful force affecting the formation of internal locus of control, we can authoritatively say that parents have a powerful opportunity to assure that their children will exhibit and experience these qualities throughout their lives. Let's explore these ideas further.

Consider family stability. "Family stability," generally defined as whether or not there is a father in the home, appears to have a significant impact on internal control. Research shows that where there is no father, children tend to be more external.[1] The family's authority style and behavior patterns also appear to influence internal control. As mentioned earlier, families where children are allowed be autonomous, to make decisions, to be dependent on themselves, and to take individual action are families that foster internality,[2] whereas families in which there is intense patriarchal authority and dominance foster externality.[3] As also mentioned earlier, children from lower socioeconomic conditions are also more often external,[4] something hypothesized by researchers to be caused by the fact that children from poor homes have fewer life opportunities. However, we also know that parental attitude and behavior has some slight effect: if parents are Internals their children will tend to be Internals as well.

This sends a clear message to parents to maintain as stable a family situation as possible and to develop a family culture where children are allowed and encouraged to exercise a reasonable degree of autonomy, are required to be independent, are held responsible for their actions, and are involved in decision making. The family should also attempt maintain a "reasonable economic level" and model internal attitudes and behaviors. When we as parents create this kind of environment for our children, we are encouraging them to live lives that are more internal than external.

With that said, my research has proven to me that parents can also *teach* internal control directly to their children. This is important to bear in mind because it is not always within the direct control of parents to ensure a "stable family" or to maintain a "reasonable economic level." But parents *can* teach the Personal Achievement Strategy and in doing so overcome deficiencies and enhance the overall internality of their children.

The family environment presents many situations and opportunities for teaching the Personal Achievement Strategy, I suggest a few here that you might consider.

Family trips. Family trips provide excellent opportunities for working through the entire Personal Achievement Strategy. It's easy to involve the children in discussions about where they'd like to go and what they'd like to do and the dialog can be fun and bonding for everyone. Setting your trip's goals and parameters can be almost as exciting as the trip itself and is educational to boot. Or perhaps you'd like to lead a group discussion with the whole entire family in attendance by having a chalkboard or a piece of newsprint on which to write your children's thoughts and suggestions. Planning and assigning responsibilities helps everyone feel a part of the enterprise as well because they will feel they have been influential in the planning process. Remembering or "evaluating" the trip afterward by looking at pictures and memorabilia and by recalling memorable experiences is another way to keep the family time together pleasant and interactive and at the same time teach a strategy step. Ahhh, the best of times.

Personal conferences. Consider establishing a weekly pattern that includes a personal conference. Many families, like mine, made Sunday night the key time to turn off the television. First, our children were expected to go to their rooms and check and finish their homework. Then, if they had nothing else to do, they were expected to read a selection of their own and think about the coming week. At this time, my wife and I made an effort to meet with them one on one to discuss what they were thinking and how they were doing. It was a perfect time to discuss goals, achievements, and plans, and to evaluate their behavior with them. But remember please, your objective is to help *them* organize their lives, decide what *they* will try to do, and gain internal control of *their* life. This time should not become an opportunity for you to tell your children what you want them to do and what you do not want them to do.

This may be as challenging for you as it was for me. I often found myself using these times to talk about things that were not going so well. "Your grades are poor in spelling. I expect you to improve." "I want you to change your attitude and your behavior toward your sister...or else!" "Do X....or Y...or Z." In these situations I was the dominating imperious father figure, insisting on my own agenda. If I could do it over again, I would try to take some additional steps. Although I might not hesitate to specify the problem behavior, to state my evaluation and displeasure, and to lay out the possible consequences that would occur in response to the behavior, now I would also: (1) ask them for their own evaluation of the behavior; (2) ask them if they want to change; and (3) ask them what they would try to do about the behavior. I would then help them set a goal of moderate risk, remembering to praise and offer support for their intended positive action. Again, the goal is to put *them* in charge, to help *them* determine and control their own behavior, to assist *them* in thinking through their situation and their behavior, and to help *them* decide to become inner-directed agents.

Conferences with my children were also opportunities to recognize accomplishments and celebrate achievements. As these conferences became a weekly pattern, my children began to anticipate them and to raise their own topics such as our treatment of them, what we were doing as a family, and what they would like to see happen in the family. As the years passed and they grew into adolescents, they began to share and discuss issues and concerns about their interactions with their peers. We discussed drinking, drugs, and sexual behavior, as well as what they were going to try to do and the way they wanted to behave. This helped them feel that they were valued members of the family and that they were able to influence their situation. This contributed to their overall sense of control.

I believe that these conversations set the pattern for my ongoing conversations with my children as adults and are one of the reasons that my children and I remain good friends today. I am grateful that they continue to share their lives with me in conversations at least once a week. Wonderful!

You can set up your own pattern of conferences. A good time to talk is just after your children have gotten into bed. This a quiet time, a time for thoughtful, low-pressure conversation. Some families have family meetings. We did not do this, but we often utilized the time when we were traveling in the car to a destination such as their grandparents' house to talk as a family. The point is that establishing times and situations when you can communicate with your children and coach them to take internal control of their lives will reap rewards that are great for both them and you.

Journaling. If I were raising children today, I would insist that they engage in some form of journaling. One of my children began keeping a journal when she was still young, in elementary school. Her initial entries were very short: "Today was a good day." "I did a good thing today." The entries became more sophisticated over time, of course, but the point here is that journaling can start at a very early age and is a way to start children thinking objectively about themselves and evaluating their actions. I suggest that you have your children make lists of their achievements and keep them in a journal; if appropriate, they can even decide to put the list on their wall. You can help them build their list by making suggestions and teach them to use the list to build their confidence as they aspire to attain new goals. The same can be done for personal strengths and interests.

You can influence your children to set goals and write them out in their journals. For several years, as the school year ended in the spring I required my children to write goals for the summer months: What did they intend to accomplish this summer? How many books did they hope to read? Did they plan to work on their swimming? Volunteer at the hospital? Wow, did I get resistance at first! But eventually my children began to take ownership of the ideas that they wrote down "just to satisfy Dad." We began talking about what they were doing and why. It was a time when I could help them plan and achieve and, at the same time, teach them about setting medium-risk goals and being specific, and the process worked very well.

Journaling or some form of journaling becomes a life-long habit for many people and is an effective method for creating and enhancing internal control. Teach this behavior and your children will be the life-long beneficiaries.

To-do lists. I live by my to-do list. If I think of something I should do, I deal with it immediately by putting it on my to-do list. At least one of my children has picked up this behavior from my modeling. Functioning with a to-do list is the day to day, down-and-dirty way for me to maintain control of my life. I do it with the context of my goals, reviewing what I can cross off at the end of the day and making a new list for the next day. This helps me stay focused during the day and move effectively from task to task. My to-do list is what I call my "cognitive steering wheel" because it enables me to respond to the serial events of the day in a controlled manner. (There is a lot of helpful literature on this practice under the term "time management,[5] so consider checking it out.)

Of course hindsight is always 20/20, but again, if I were raising my children now I would require them to keep to-do lists in some modified format. I did this modestly as a teacher in that I required my students to keep a list of their homework assignments. With my children at home, it was, "Okay, get your homework list out. Let's see where you are." Consider having a family to-do list on the wall, where each family task is listed, followed by a name. Remember, being in control of one's life means in part being organized. Being organized means knowing what you need to do, when, and why. A to-do list enables you and your children to be effective and efficient.

Model this list behavior. Give your child the advantage of focus and goal orientation at least some of the time. You will begin to see the contrast between your children and other children who have no focus or agenda, are lackadaisical, respond to impulse, are easily influenced by others, seldom finish a task, forget what they are supposed to do, and often don't even start to do any work. Help your children learn to thoughtfully plan and structure their day and to experience the joy and satisfaction in doing it. Talk about doing the planning in just that way. Share the feelings and excitement of structuring and controlling one's life to get things done!

Community activities. Some community, non-school activities are ideal for teaching the Personal Achievement Strategy. Consider involving your children in some organization like scouting, for example. Scouting has a ladder of achievement that invites children to learn specific knowledge, use their skills, develop worthwhile attitudes, and have great experiences while they learn. Children set goals and advance based on their own interests and efforts. Because the program encourages parents to work with their children in setting and achieving these goals, you can help your child plan and motivate himself to do the tasks required. Camping experience in which the children are responsible for the camp tasks has been shown to increase internal control of the participants, one great reason for seeking out these kinds of programs and making use of these tailor-made opportunities to teach and nurture internal control.

Sports. Sport programs offer an excellent opportunity to teach the Personal Achievement Strategy. Most children at one time or another are interested in engaging in one sport or another, and there are many attractive structured opportunities for participation, like little league, basketball, and so on. When a child first begins to participate in a sports program she has little knowledge of the game, its rules, and so on. But after some experience she will begin to get the lay of the land and soon to formulate hopes and dreams. She might want to be a good dribbler or he might want to be a striker. He might want to be able to throw or hit the ball in baseball. But at this point children have little idea of what they can do to affect their performance. Many think, as I did when I was young, that some people have it and some don't and that success in sports is a gift, a matter of sheer luck…that if you don't have the knack it's just too bad.

This is where you, the parent, can step in because even a little training and practice will help. One suggestion is to get a book on the sport that interests your child and talk about what beginners can do to begin to improve. Talk with your child and see if he wants to work on improving. It's *his* decision; does he want to try? Set a modest goal with him to try working on a skill, say batting or throwing a baseball. There are CDs that illustrate the mechanics of these skills. Get one. Watch it with your child. Suggest she practice the moves, the patterns. Play a game of catch with her and maybe a friend. Make sure it's *play*. Then evaluate with your child. Does he see any improvement? What else does she think she can do to improve? Does she want to continue? If so, set a new goal and begin to plan.

I have served as a Little League coach and I have coached soccer. I have observed both parents and children stunned by the rate of advance after just a little bit of effort on the child's part to practice and improve. Once that happens, the child and the parent become excited and really begin to focus and work. "Hey, we can influence our own performance," the children realize, and soon they're off and running. In some cases there is such a transformation that they continue to practice in the off season and show up the next year significantly improved and ready to participate at a much higher level. Now they are clearly on the upward spiral of

achievement > increasing internal control > achievement

Athletic performance is not a given. This means anyone can exercise at least a degree of control over his or her athletic performance. Athletic success has a powerful effect on the life of the child, and we know that adolescent social success and even academic performance correlate with athletic performance. The message to our youth? If you put in the effort to become a good player you can change your social standing, improve your grades, and feel good about yourself.

Parental role. There are many possible situations that offer the opportunity to learn and employ the Personal Achievement Strategy. Musical education is one; school themes and projects are another. But note well, parents, *you have a key role.* You must also be a player. You must commit time, energy, and thought to interacting with your child. As we've said, the best way to prepare yourself to teach the Personal Achievement Strategy to your children is to learn to use it and understand the details of its application yourself. You do not need to hover or harass, however.

Just a little effort in the right places at the right time can be significant and the payoff for your children will be enormous!

2. Addiction rehabilitation. Addition rehabilitation is another area where teaching the Personal Achievement Strategy can likely be extremely beneficial. This is because the positive qualities of internal control directly address the negative qualities of the addictive personality. Consider the following lists comparing the negative characteristics of the addictive personality (on the left) and the research documented positive characteristics of the Internal (on the right).

Characteristics of the addictive (externally controlled) personality	Characteristics of the internally controlled personality
Exhibits lack of interest in self-development and in the future	Active in self-development and future-oriented
Relies on external sources for self-identity and prestige	Defines one's own worth and being self-assertive
Feels alienated from home, school, and society	Engages in and is active in the community
Feels a sense of powerlessness, normlessness, and isolation	Demonstrates personal agency and responsibility
Engages in high-risk behavior	Engages in medium-risk behavior
Exhibits a low-value rating relative to enlightenment, skills, affection, respect, power, and rectitude	Exhibits a high-value rating to learning, responsibility, and ethical behavior

The addictive personality is the very definition of externality. Or, said in reverse, most everything the Internal is, the addictive personality is not. For this reason alone, any drug therapy training program should give consideration to incorporating the Personal Achievement Strategy into its curriculum.

3. Basic life skills for the mentally and emotionally impaired. "Life skills" refer to a wide range of knowledge and skills believed to be essential for adult living (Brolin, 1989). At present, many people who are physically challenged have special needs that have to be addressed. These individuals require education and support to learn these necessary life behaviors. The three major life-skill areas that need to be addressed are daily living, personal/social skills, and occupational skills. For example, even when one is physically challenged in some way, valuable skills include dressing and grooming oneself properly, using appropriate table manners, making decisions about money, and using public transportation.

Most lists of life skills include decision making, self-confidence-building skills, and positive thinking,[7] behaviors that we know are also integral aspects of the Personal Achievement Strategy. As such, the strategy can be said to directly address the needs of these challenged populations. Of course, life skills need to be individually modified for different disabilities, age, severity of disability, and life expectation. For example, life-skill goals for the blind need to be defined differently from those for the deaf or the emotional disturbed.

Physically challenged individuals are most often external by nature.[8] This is as we might expect, particularly since they have repeatedly been made aware that they are inadequate; that they are "less." Hence, they are often devastated and depressed by their place in the world. But these individuals need not be live their lives as Externals. Those who work with the disabled note that sometimes there are individuals who buck the norm, who behave with much more internality than their external counterparts to perform effectively within the limits of their disabilities. For example, within any given challenged population there will be those who work at learning to manage their money, while others give up even though they might learn the same behavior with effort.

I recently read about a man who had no arms. Certainly we might expect that having no arms would dispose most of us to feel inadequate, discouraged, and dependent, and to behave externally. However, this man, Liu Wei, won the *China's Got Talent* competition with his piano rendition of the James Blunt song *You're Beautiful.*[9] How? Liu Wei played the piano with his toes!! Is this man an Internal or what??!! We might ask the same of Helen Keller. The point is that disabled individuals can learn to become internal within the limits of their disability—and it is important and valuable for them to do so.

I have a friend, we'll call her "Anne," who is the administrator for 17 group homes for adults who are unable to live on their own and need support for their emotional disabilities. The clients live in a typical house that has been modified for several adults. Each home has live-in staff members who are on the premises most of the time and who monitor and support the clients. Food is provided and the clients are encouraged to go into the community on their own as they are able. Anne has suggested to me that the Personal Achievement Strategy could be taught as a way of behaving and working together for both the clients and the staff. She finds that a major problem for most of the clients is their lack of confidence. They have no sense of control and they expect to fail. This is depressing for the clients and frustrating for the staff, who are trying to teach them and nurture them.

Anne has indicated that she is particularly taken with the way the Personal Achievement Strategy begins. She believes that it would be very helpful and confirming for her clients to develop lists of past achievements and strengths. She believes that having staff work with clients to build these lists would help bond and energize both groups. She envisions every client having a list of strengths and past achievements on the wall of his room. She believes that generating goal ideas and setting goals could work with this challenged population. She believes that the Personal Achievement Strategy can also provide a process structure for the staff to work together with the clients as well as to help the clients achieve their goals. Together the staff and the clients could look forward to addressing the future with hope and purpose. They could develop individual personal plans with specific goals. This would predictably lead to higher morale both for staff and for clients, which in turn would lead to a more effective and efficient operation of the organization.

As of this writing Anne is considering introducing the strategy on a low-risk basis. She is thinking of teaching it to both staff and clients in one or two homes to see how it works, and to learn how it can best be utilized. Then, if it seems feasible and productive, she will consider instituting the internal control training in the other homes under her supervision. It will be interesting to see how this plan works out.

Note that I entitled this section "*basic* life skills." That is because I suggest that any list of life skills in the future be conceptually reorganized. The Personal Achievement Strategy should be considered basic and should be implemented along with the other life skills; in this way it would become the fundamental process for learning and employing all the rest of those skills. I suggest that the Personal Achievement Strategy be a primary focus of any life-skills program of instruction.

4. Juniata College: ICS design in use. The ideas and spirit of the Personal Achievement Strategy have been employed by Juniata College for a period of 40 years. When you speak to graduates of Juniata College who matriculated after 1973 and ask them, "What was your POE?" you see them light up. POE is the campus shorthand, or acronym, for "Program of Emphasis." As soon as these graduates start to talk about their POE, you feel their excitement and passion, even though they participated in the program many years before. You might ask, "Oh, you mean your major?" "No," they say, "it's kind of like that…only different."

Let's explore what that means.

During their initial years at Juniata, students are required to define a program of studies to be their focus, their POE. Unique and unusual ideas are welcome and considered; traditional study programs are also welcome. The distinction is that the college shifts the responsibility for decision making and scheduling to the students in order to empower them. In doing this, Juniata College has evolved a curriculum model that utilizes the ideas and principles of internal control training.

In order to convey the structure and the spirit of the Juniata curriculum I am going to quote the college literature directly below, because I believe this literature conveys what I want to communicate better than I can. Here is the lead-in in Juniata College's principle recruitment publication. Catch the spirit as well as the thought.

> For many students, their range or mix of interests complicates choice of an academic focus. They need this one opportunity to explore their interests before choosing one over others.
>
> That's what exploration is all about. About 15 percent of the students that come to Juniata start out as what we call exploratory—they've not yet declared a

specific Program of Emphasis, or POE. Some colleges call that "undecided," a designation that strikes us as unfair. We know that you are seeking options, seeking to make good choices, looking to find the field or subjects that inspire and motivate you. After testing your interests, you may decide that you don't want to choose, you want to combine. At Juniata, the POE encourages you to do this, and you can still graduate in four years.

So, you have come to the right place. Juniata faculty and students revel in exploration, in hands-on experience, in curiosity and drive and passion—to explore the world, to engage it—to think, evolve, and act.

The recruitment publication goes on to make the following points:

Juniata's distinct Program of Emphasis enables students to personalize their education. Working with two advisers, students can design an academic program around their interests and plans, for a more meaningful educational experience. Students may elect to follow an already designed program of study selected from a list of approved, or "designated," POEs, but half of all Juniata students design their own POEs.

As you can see, Juniata casts perspective students as searchers, explorers, and agents from the initial contact. The college follows through by stimulating students to engage in planning their own Program of Emphasis from the very beginning. There is a special freshman course devoted to program exploration, and each student is assigned two or more advisers with whom to work throughout their college career. There is a structured schedule of decisions that the students and their advisers move through as they progress from semester to semester. For example, students are required to develop a tentative POE by the end of the first year. Then, in the second year, they are required to have a firm POE laid out with a course plan and advisors in place. In the following years students are invited to re-access and re-plan as they proceed.

Juniata offers a supporting structure of courses and student services available to each student. This includes opportunities for self-study, career and graduate school planning, and assistance with obtaining POE-related internships. There is a clearly defined process for developing and obtaining approval of student POEs. "Want to combine the study of Mathematics and Theater Performance...Accounting and Environmental Studies...maybe even Biology and Ethics?" You are welcomed, encouraged, and supported in your pursuits at Juniata. You will be assisted in selecting appropriate courses, in obtaining hands-on related experiences, and in participating in internships related to your POE.

Students who do not chose to select an already prescribed POE are responsible for developing their own POE plan, including courses and internship experiences and presenting this POE proposal to the College Curriculum Committee. Students who follow this path also write a rationale supporting their interest and commitment to their unique POE. The Curriculum Committee uses the following criteria to determine acceptance or rejection of the proposed POE: (1) coherence of the program; (2) evidence of study in-depth; and (3) if interdisciplinary, relationship of the courses to a specific objective. If the Committee approves, the student is empowered and supported in going forward to pursue his or her personally formulated learning objective.

This college-wide process creates a climate of student responsibility, a low-level buzz that permeates the learning community. Here is a quote from a recent freshman:

Simply living in this amazing academic community while being able to have a completely open mind about what my POE will be has helped me considerably. Being "exploratory" has enabled me to focus on my current studies while making mental notes about potential POEs for the future, yet not committing to any of these just yet.

Here is a quote from an upper-class woman:

Since Child Life Studies isn't a designated POE, my advisers and I are working together to choose the right classes and internships that will enable me to become a child life specialist or go on to graduate school.

There are many, many examples like these, all testifying to the positive experiences, pride, and excitement that graduates still feel about their POE experiences. I recently met a graduate who had combined an emphasis on Spanish culture and language together with premed, and who is today the power figure in an inner city medical clinic in Baltimore. She praises her experience at Juniata which allowed and supported her in pursuing these two interests. Another recent graduate combined a rigorous health-care program with an emphasis on political science. I call that a study curriculum to meet today's needs, don't you? This young woman immediately found a job in Washington D.C. and is on her way.

A list of the POEs of the current seniors provides us with many examples of just how unique they are. Here are just a few:

- Brain and language studies with a secondary emphasis in mathematics
- Business and animal behavior
- Communications and religious studies

- Environment and decision economics
- Philosophy and earth sciences
- Theater and peace studies
- User-centered informatics with a secondary emphasis in philosophy
- Theater performance with a secondary emphasis in marketing
- Sociology and legal studies

Learners at Juniata are clearly empowered and required to take responsibility for their own learning in this environment. Juniata's POE curriculum structure has been in place for 40 years; in its original conceptualization, internal locus of control was a dominant guiding principle. I know because I was actively involved in its initial planning. The Juniata faculty has since codified the program and has created a defined structure, supporting programs, and trained personnel to enable the program to function successfully. The current program design is the result of repeated evaluations and adjustments, and all the steps of the strategy are applied in multiple ways. As such, it offers a model for the design of a teaching/learning program that embodies the concepts of internal control training.

This focus on empowering learners contrasts with other undergraduate programs where the emphasis might be on the quality of the faculty, the eminence of the departments, or campus social life. The preeminent emphasis on development of the learner as an internally directed agent is in keeping with Juniata's motto: *Think, Evolve, Act.*

5. The black-white achievement gap. For more than 100 years national testing has documented a very substantial achievement gap between white and black children in both mathematics and reading.[10] Many educational programs that have been mounted focus on eliminating this gap. Major national policy efforts, such as the current "No Child Left Behind Initiative," are devoted to closing this disparity. And though this substantial gap between black and white has narrowed slightly, it continues to exist to a great extent today.

Researchers have studied the causes of this persisting achievement gap for many years and have identified as many as 16 factors that they hypothesize have some causal effect.[11] For whatever reason, perhaps because they are sociologists rather than psychologists, they neglect to mention locus of control as a factor. However, I look to the *Coleman Report*, which does identify internal control and related attitudes as the major factor explaining variations in children's achievement.[12]

In their research, Coleman and others (1966) found that there was a substantial gap in the difference between black children and white children in their internal-external attitudes. Afro-American children scored as Externals much more often than white children, correlating directly with the achievement levels of the testing sample of the 150,000 children in the study. Black children who were poor and from inner city poverty neighborhoods predictably scored as Externals and scored low on the achievement measures. Even black children who lived in upscale suburban neighborhoods and scored external scored low on the achievement measures.

But here's the really interesting thing: Coleman also found that when a black child scored as an Internal, whether or not s/he came from an inner city neighborhood, was at the poverty level, or even came from an unstable family environment, this black child achieved at or above the level of white children!!!

Hmm...shocking? As you know after reading the previous chapters of this book, we have evidence showing that we know how to teach children to be more internal. Therefore, do you think?...Is it possible?...that explicitly teaching black children to be internal could result in a significant gain in achievement? This is quite a stretch. Could teaching the Personal Achievement Strategy really negate the lifetime influences of a child's culture? Maybe. Let me hasten to state that teaching internal locus of control will most probably not compensate for all of the deprivations suffered by black children. Nor is teaching internal locus of control a magic bullet.

But it does appear that it might be a significant factor. It may help us move in the right direction.

Fortunately, we can resolve this question empirically. In other words, we can create a research design that will enable us to confirm or deny the hypothesis that teaching children to be internal will result in increases in mathematical and reading achievement. Is this worth a try? I think so.

Consider this tentative proposal. There are a number of after-school programs that supplement and bolster the education of disadvantaged learners. In the main, these programs are run by nonprofit agencies and churches at off-school locations. The administrators of these programs have leeway in how the programs are designed. Typically these programs include the following components: a snack and recreation period, periodic large group presentations, field trips, guidance and career coaching, and subject instruction in mathematics, writing, reading, and computer use. Could we not utilize these programs to teach and test the effectiveness of the Personal Achievement Strategy?

First, we need to obtain both the cooperation of the administrators of several of these after-school programs and the cooperation of the school districts where the children of these programs attend school. Then the research design is set up as follows:

Step 1. Children in each after-school program are randomly placed in "treatment" and "non-treatment" groups. The non-treatment groups participate in the programs in which they would normally participate as part of their after-school programs. The treatment groups receive training and practice in using the Personal Achievement Strategy. The groups are controlled for significant variables that might make the groups uneven.

Step 2. The internal control group training continues throughout the year. The members of the treatment group are led to use the Personal Achievement Strategy in different domains, such as interpersonal relations and athletic activities, and in repeated applications to school subjects. Measurements for attitude and other behaviors are administered in the same way that the research study discussed in Chapter 5 was administered. The objective is to document that the members of the treatment group learn to use the strategy and move toward being more internal.

Step 3. Math and reading achievement test scores and other related behaviors of both the treatment and non-treatment groups, such as school marks, are then tracked for a period of three or more years following the completion of the instructional year. In order to do this the cooperation of each school district is necessary. During this period the children predictably participate in some statewide and district-wide measures of reading and math. If not, perhaps arrangements are made to administer a battery of math and reading measures to the learners who are participating in the research study.

By comparing the achievement of the treatment group and the alternate treatment group we can confirm or deny our hypothesis: that teaching internal control will result in increases in math and reading achievement.

I invite anyone who can marshal the resources to carry out a study like the one I have sketched out here to do it. Count on me for any help you may require. In the meantime, I will be trying to mount and carry out a similar research effort.

6. A process guide for volunteer groups, marriages, and corporations. The Personal Achievement Strategy is a productive process guide for task groups. Want to pull a group together, get them organized and fired up to get something done? The Personal Achievement Strategy is the process guide that works. Let's play with this idea. Let's think about how one might use the strategy in three different situations: a volunteer committee, a marriage, and a small corporation.

A. Volunteer groups. Suppose you are appointed to chair a task group in your religious congregation and are charged with doing something about the problem of homeless families in your community. The members of your committee are scratching their heads. "What can we do? We're not social workers. We're just ordinary people with busy lives to live." How would you start?

Let's role play the situation.

Right off the bat people in these types of circumstances, people start working with a process pattern that is problem-focused—that is, using the typical problem-solving model. This makes sense: define and study the problem and then consider alternative proposals for the solution. Problem solving begins with study and convergent thinking, where you focus on the problem or the barriers and on how the barriers can be overcome. Actually, I was taught to do the same thing.

In contrast, the Personal Achievement Strategy begins with a focus on the task group and its supporting institution—*not on the problem.* The strategy focuses on the past achievements, strengths, and interests of the task group and the congregation.

Hmm…how does that make logical sense? Don't we need to look at the problem, not at ourselves and how good we are? Maybe, but maybe not. Maybe it makes psychological or emotive sense. Let's explore further.

In my experience what happens with most problem-solving groups is that they continue to focus more and more tightly on the problem and on evaluating alternative solutions. As conversation remain centered on the problem and the barriers, the group naturally shrinks to a few dedicated people. The enthusiasm and energy level drops. The affective climate becomes cooler, if not cold. Group discussions become increasingly cognitive and logical. And although the group may produce an excellent penetrating analysis and an innovative proposal for a solution, what happens to the action? The group's proposed alternative may be brilliant, but often it will be too demanding and require too much time and energy from busy people. The deliberations take on a constrictive quality; there may be clarity, but not a lot of momentum to carry things through. Sure, this problem-solving approach may have defined the problem and specified the plan, but now the energy and commitment that has been lost must be rebuilt…renewed…in order for any action to occur. Is there anyone left at this point who is still willing to expend the energy to follow the plan? Maybe… Hopefully...

In contrast, the Personal Achievement Strategy begins by *building* energy and optimism from the onset along with the belief that group members can and will act. It does this by having its members recall their past achievements and the strengths of their congregation as a group and as individuals, which invites ongoing participation. As the desire to participate grows among the members of the group, so does their belief in the possibility of significant accomplishment. Recalling what they have successfully accomplished in the past also suggests the doable limits of their ensuing goal ideas. Using this information about themselves helps further define the task and generate alternatives. The group members *see* themselves doing what they plan.

In essence, the Personal Achievement Strategy not only deals with the cognitive and procedural aspects of mounting effective action, but also addresses the emotive affective aspects of effective action.

Am I saying that the Personal Achievement Strategy is a better process guide than the problem-solving approach or some other model? Not necessarily. But it is an alternative worth considering. The strategy is distinctive in that it looks to manage the group's affect as well as logical process. If the task group is characterized by a strong direct command and control structure, the problem-solving approach may work quite well. But if the task group is composed of volunteers, where continual buy-in of the participants is necessary, the Personal Achievement Strategy may be your best bet.

I have had success in employing this strategy in groups and organizations by leading participants to achieve and gain greater control of their environment. It is noteworthy that I have also employed the strategy to develop organizations that continue to serve the homeless of many communities.

B. Marriages and partnerships. The Personal Achievement Strategy can work wonders in a marriage relationship or partnership. The first necessity is a commitment for the partners to take the time to talk at designated times about the strategy steps. This can be pillow time, driving-together time, or time over a quiet dinner. What's important is that partners talk about their achievements, their strengths, and their interests together. They share goal ideas, what would excite them to work on together. Think of how this kind of interaction stimulates a complimentary approach and supportiveness and encouragement! And later how it will be reinforced by some warm . . . well, you know. The real point is that when instituted as described the strategy has a positive emotive effect that causes individuals to go forward in responsive, dedicated ways to make their desires, hopes, and dreams come true. Remember, since the focus is not on perceived *problems*, there is no "hangover," the detritus of negativity, either.

Additionally, using the strategy allows for the development of a process for communication and decision making, one that deals with and ameliorates the issues of power and control in any relationship. Partners talk about what they want to do together and the kind of relationship that they want to build. The climate is warm and loving. They listen, they hear and honor their partner and their partner listens to, hears, and honors them. Communication of this nature helps to avoid the head-to-head power-position taking that so often creates an atmosphere of win-lose and adversity, possibly even anger and hate.

But that's not all! Step 3, that of setting a goal, is not only a cognitive function, but an emotional action. It has the gravitas of a "commitment." Partners who set a goal together are committing to taking responsibility, to caring, to action, and to making themselves accountable to themselves. Making the decision to work together to attain this goal is weighty...exciting... bonding.

Does this require that problems of, say, money, be ignored? No. But utilizing the strategy (1) creates a positive environment; (2) creates a process for addressing and resolving the issues, possibly even from a win-win perspective; and (3) creates a situation that allows participants to deal with the problem within the larger context of their joint commitment to future goals. And, as mentioned earlier, couples learn to "flip" specific problem issues into specific goal statements that they can now work together to achieve.

But this is not all! Strategy Step 5 is to strive. This is a highly motivating time, when feeling, energy, focus, and drive are required to get it done. This presents partners with a wonderful opportunity to love and support and interact with each other. They begin to see that they really *can* make a difference to one another. This can happen even if the specified goal is the other partner's, because the each is identifying with the other. When even one individual is supportive and encouraging, it is extremely rewarding. Personally, the times I spent with my wife in this way are some of the warmest and most gratifying memories of my 50-year marriage. I wish the same for you.

I recommend partners start by discussing the strategy's first step by listing their past accomplishments together, their own individual strengths, and then their partner's strengths, as well as the strengths they feel they have in combination. Then partners can discuss how to build on all these positive attributes, ideas, and actions. Believe me when I say that people who implement this effort never go back.

C. Corporations. Suppose you are the CEO of a small corporation of about 300 employees and your company makes the ubiquitous widgets. Let's make the situation really difficult, though. You have just been hired by the board to follow a CEO who was fired. Your charge: Make more money.

How will you approach this situation? You are an experienced CEO. You have been successful in managing other corporations; this is why you were hired. One way to begin is by introducing yourself to your staff, assuring them that you have been successful in other enterprises and that you intend to be successful in this one. You then lay out the policies and procedures you want them to follow and what you want them to do. You establish a structure of management and accountability and proceed to enforce your plan.

I have seen this kind of approach work well. I have seen this kind of approach result in a total revolt. I have seen this approach work poorly because of masked hostility, lack of buy-in, and lethargy; how it can lead to weak performance because the CEO is attempting to apply previous methods that may have worked elsewhere to his new corporation, not recognizing that his new company is different and requires the application of different methods.

The Personal Achievement Strategy process offers another alternative. In this approach the CEO again introduces himself to his new staff and assures them that he has been successful in other enterprises and that he intends to be successful here. But post-introduction he takes a different fork in the road. This time the CEO then asks his new staff for their help in understanding the corporation. He holds discussions in which the staff and the workers become involved in identifying past achievements and strengths. The CEO publicly acknowledges these past achievements and strengths and the people associated with them. He continues to work with the staff to develop goal ideas, both for general and specific functions of the organization. He develops plans with his employees to achieve these goals. He moves forward with the support of his workers.

Although initially this approach does not appear to be as dynamic and assertive as the first approach our CEO has taken, in the end it can work extremely well. Yes, it takes more time and fuss. Because he is not telling people what to do and requiring them to do it, he may get a lot of noise as a result and find himself spending more time listening than he would like. But he is also offering everyone in his company dignity, recognition, and opportunity. He will learn information about the organization and the personnel that may otherwise take years to learn—if he ever learns it. Mobilizing and focusing his employees on the objectives of his—and their—enterprise builds motivation, morale, and buy-in. He is empowering them and influencing them to think and act in a way that will predictably increase the efficiency and effectiveness of the whole organization.

I have seen this approach work in schools, hospitals, and sales organizations. Again, the Personal Achievement Strategy is not just a guide to a logical procedure, but an interweaving of logic with a psychological emotive thread that contributes to the process of achieving desired goals. This strategy is effective for managing enterprises as well as for managing one's personal behavior.

7. School application. Let's begin our discussion of how we might apply the teaching of the Personal Achievement Strategy in our schools by reviewing the research relating academic achievement and internal locus of control.

The principle purpose of schools is to foster academic achievement. True, schools are tasked with many other objectives, including mental health, physical health, and even driver safety, but there is unequivocal agreement that their primary purpose is to foster academic achievement.

Internal locus of control clearly and robustly correlates with academic achievement. Academic achievers exhibit internal control and those who exhibit internal control exhibit academic achievement. The academic achievement of Internals is documented by many studies in many ways ranging from superior standardized test scores and superior school performance to the more frequent completion of academic programs of study and more (see Academic Achievement in Chapter 2).

Moreover, as reported above, J. S. Coleman's study of 150,000 learners states that "a pupil factor, which appears to have a stronger relationship to achievement than do all the 'school' factors taken together, is the extent which an individual feels that he has control over his own destiny." Further, the researchers found that "the child's sense of control of their environment is most strongly related to achievement" and that internal locus of control overrides the effect of race, gender, social class, economic level, and family stability. Consequently, if you are a school leader or administrator and are serious about encouraging academic achievement in your schools, you must give serious consideration to initiating a school-wide effort to teach internal locus of control.

Given this unequivocal imperative, how then can we employ the Personal Achievement Strategy in our schools to teach internal control for the benefit of our youth? It's one thing to teach the strategy once (as described in Chapter 5), but we know that learners must continue using the strategy or lose it. We want our children to be internally directed in ongoing academic achievement activities through out their school years. How might this be accomplished?

Outlining. In order to answer this question, I suggest we look to an analogue offered by how we teach another abstract intellectual skill, that of "outlining." Outlining is an important foundation for many other essential academic skills. It is an important part of reading comprehension, note taking, summarizing, studying, action planning, and writing composition. Most school curriculums introduce outlining at about the fifth-grade level due to judgments about developmental intellectual readiness. At first outlining is taught as a skill in itself. Then teachers begin to use it and coach its use repeatedly in different subject areas like science, reading skill lessons, writing composition, and history. Teachers come to expect learners to know and use this basic intellectual skill throughout the rest of their educational program. Outline skills become a basic cognitive tool that learners employ in a wide range of academic domains. I suggest that the Personal Achievement Strategy be taught and employed much in the same manner throughout the learner's school career.

What follows are my suggestions for phasing in the utilization of this strategy into a school program. These suggestions are directed to principals. Again, these ideas are just suggestions. It's your school, and you need to do it your way. But do it!

Assuming that you have developed teacher understanding and buy-in regarding the exploratory use of the Personal Achievement Strategy, I suggest that you begin by instituting time for learners to use the strategy three times a week, perhaps on Mondays, Wednesdays, and Fridays. This is relatively easy to do, especially in a self-contained elementary school classroom, though it will probably take some scheduling adaptation in a secondary school. It can be justified as a part of a guidance program.

In this situation, learners are taught to use the strategy in the beginning weeks of the school year. Soon they begin applying the strategy to set and achieve real goals in their lives on a weekly schedule. After the initial instructional period, the classes settle into a weekly routine for sessions related to getting goal ideas, setting goals, and planning. Mondays and Wednesdays serve as check-in times. How are things going? How is the striving going? Do you need to re-plan? Where are you in your planning sequence? Fridays serve as evaluation days.

Learners are required to keep journals. In addition to information and notes about homework and other day-to-day school business, a section of these journals is set aside for working on their use of the strategy, to set goals, generate goal ideas, and so on. This is a good place for keeping a list of past achievements, strengths, and interests, as well as evaluations of their efforts to achieve their goals. Teachers should make it clear that they will have access to at least part of each learner's journal for monitoring, guiding, and coaching purposes.

The Teacher's Role. Now let's discuss the teacher's role. Teachers who are teaching the Personal Achievement Strategy are expected to: teach the use of the strategy and encourage its use by individual learners to set and work on their own goals; serve as coaches to their learners by assisting them to utilize the strategy for their school work and in other domains, as appropriate; and serve as group developers. In this case, the teacher leads and facilitates group sharing of individual goals, striving efforts, and achievements on a regular schedule with the objective of developing a supportive group climate, where learners are sharing, helping each other, and caring about each other. Groups like these hopefully become the learners' emotional base as they progress through school.

The Principal's Role. The principal's role is to encourage and support the teachers in teaching the strategy and encouraging learners to use the strategy in their academic activities. This might include continuing instruction, suggestions, and occasional discussions around the kinds of things the teachers are doing. It might also include evaluating whether teaching the strategy is making a difference in behavior and achievement levels in the school. If the teacher comments reported in the evaluation study in Chapter 5 can be taken as an indication, teachers should be reporting that the learners are more organized, more confident, work together better as a class, and have better discussion skills.

You as the principal can also make a significant contribution by mounting a school-wide effort to promote the use of the strategy. This might consist of putting up posters and other visuals referring to the strategy with appropriate sayings or about striving or reaching goals. You might promote class activities, such as having art classes create collages of achievers and hanging them in the halls. I know you will have many, many ideas, and I encourage you to try them all.

It's always helpful to recognize exemplary uses of the strategy, too. Who are the achievers? What unusual things are individual learners achieving in and out of school? Encourage the achievers to talk about their goal setting, perhaps by describing their thinking at the time they decided to start working on becoming a skating champion and the effort it took. Set up situations where learners communicate to their fellow learners that it is not just talent; that goal setting, planning, and drive are crucial factors in the process.

School-wide programs, such as films that illustrate many of the strategy steps, are also wonderful aids, especially if you follow the presentation with a discussion on the relevant points. Again, this is your milieu, and I know you are the one qualified to do it and do it well.

As principal, another very important aspect in implementing this strategy is to make sure to communicate with parents. Share with parents what you are trying to do, and invite them to support and participate in the school's effort to teach Internality to their children. This might involve a written communication, a meeting to introduce the concept of the Personal Achievement Strategy, and an offer of a workshop that invites parents to learn about the strategy in greater detail, in particular to learn how to coach and support their children in the use of the strategy. Like any effort to communicate with parents, it needs to be regular and ongoing. Imagine a time when teachers and parents are able to communicate about a child's use of the strategy and then work together to help that child become more internal, more self-directed, more successful in school, and to experience greater well-being and contentment. The research predicts that this will happen.

Cumulative Effects. Two or three years after introducing the use of the strategy you might begin to build its use into your evaluation program. You might go forward with this possibility once you feel your teachers are familiar with the program, when you have a parent communication program in place, and when you feel your learners fully understand what is expected of them. Have teachers evaluate each learner's use of the strategy step by step and share the evaluation with the learner as well as with the parents. If feasible, build the evaluation into the report card. Not only does this give power, authority, and value to those who teach the strategy, but it sends a very strong message to the learners that this program is important.

Let's imagine the cumulative effects of this program after three years. By this point there will be several grade levels of learners who have been using the strategy for more than a year. It is now a part of their thinking, language, and behavior. The teachers who have been teaching the strategy and using it for a period of three years are now employing its language routinely in their classes. Perhaps they are using contracts to allow their learners to set differed levels of content achievement in their classrooms. Perhaps they are using contracts to encourage extra-credit projects. Hopefully they are using the strategy to help learners carry out long-term projects and to set up and manage independent learning programs. Science projects are an obvious example of this type of effort.

After three years, parents will be aware of the centrality of the strategy in the curriculum and (hopefully) understand it. Some parents have become enthusiasts and are actively using the strategy as a part of their parenting. In summary, you now have a community that is knowledgeable and sympathetic to the use of the strategy.

With these attributes at work, what effects might we expect to see in this school? We can make some suppositions based on the research reported in Chapter 3 and the reports of the teachers in the evaluation study reported in Chapter 5. That is, if we increase internality we should see the following results:

1. Learner academic achievement improves; standardized test scores go up;
2. Learners are more organized and responsive to instruction;
3. Learners work together more effectively, exhibit group skills, and are better school citizens;
4. Learners exhibit better behavior overall; discipline problems decline;
5. Learners seem happier; school morale improves;
6. Learners experience less debilitating anxiety; emotional problems decline;
7. Learners engage in more independent learning activities;
8. Teacher morale improves; and
9. Drop-out rates decline and graduation rates improve (in secondary schools).

Will these things actually happen? My friends are pessimistic. "Russ, teaching internality—the Personal Achievement Strategy—is a great idea, but schools will never do it." But I'm not so sure. In fact, schools are teaching and employing bits and pieces of the strategy right now. Consider this quote from a recent editorial in a local newspaper.

Editorial: *Asbury Park Press*, February 18, 2011

"An 'A' in goal setting

Here is a novel idea: Have elementary school pupils participate in parent-teacher conferences by showing off their work and setting goals with their parents and teachers. The Red Bank school system began having fourth-grade students lead discussions about their progress in conjunction with their report cards with their parents and teachers. It's beyond us why more districts haven't begun making students a partner in establishing goals and discussing strategies for helping them meet those goals."

This editorial from New Jersey goes on to extol the idea of involving students in setting goals and planning to achieve them, and then congratulates the Red Bank School District for its innovative leadership. This current concrete example suggests there is wide acceptance for these ideas in schools. All we need is leadership.

Summary

I hope you've found these sketches of possible applications of the Personal Achievement Strategy to be intriguing. I hope they will inspire you to create situations in which you might teach internality. If you do decide to develop an internal control instructional program, I would love to hear from you. You can communicate with me directly through my website, teachinternalcontrol. com, where I provide support and resources and serve as a link to others who share our common interest and objectives.

I am dedicated to increasing learner Internality and empowering life-long learners.

Let's do it together.

Chapter 7

Instructional Design Format:
Teaching the Personal Achievement Strategy

In this chapter, we describe a direct classroom instructional approach in detail, one in which a specific time has been set aside for teaching the Personal Achievement Strategy. I suggest that you read this chapter *only* if you are interested the details of internal control instruction. In this format, teaching the strategy is both the instructor's and the learner's primary focus. Since the curriculum discussed in the last chapter was used with such comprehensively excellent results, we'll use it here for the purpose of making suggestions on how to teach the Personal Achievement Strategy with this instructional approach.

This curriculum design provides an overall organizational structure that will help you to think about these suggestions for teaching the strategy. Give this approach serious review. While it was created for fifth-grade children, it can easily be adapted for a wide range of learners as needed.

Figure 11: ACT program organizational structure: the Six Achievement Steps.

	1 Study Self PART 1	2 Get Goal Ideas PART 2	3 Set a Goal PART 3	4 Plan PART 4	5 Strive PART 5	6 Evaluate PART 6
UNIT I	Learn to define achivement	Draw self achieving	Learn about ACT	Learn to work in a group	Set goals and strive in a game	Learn the six achievement steps
UNIT II	Name past achievements	Get goal ideas from past achievements	Make goal specific	Name and order tasks	Use envisioning, achievement, and heroes	Decide how well you did
UNIT III	Name personal strengths	Get goal ideas from strengths	Make goal medium risk	Replan when faced with problems	Use competition	Evaluate progress with ACT
UNIT IV	Name group strengths	Get goal ideas for your group	Select a group goal	Plan tasks for group	Strive for your goal	Evaluate group achievement

In Figure 11 you can see that there are a total of 26 cells, arranged in four rows. Some of the cells incorporate several lessons. In the lessons of Unit 1, an introduction to the instructional program (the first row across), learners are introduced to the instructional program and prepared for learning to use the strategy. In the lessons of Units II and III, learners are led through two complete applications of the strategy. Unit IV lessons lead the class through the use of the strategy on a group basis. Using this format, the learners use the strategy three different times in all, twice as individuals and once as group members. Each time the learners proceed through the use of the strategy they are taught to use it more effectively.

The primary learning objectives of each lesson are stated in each of the cells. After three uses the learners have learned to use the strategy and the experience has influenced their beliefs and behavior (as discussed in Chapter 5).

. . .

We will now examine the curriculum design in closer detail, starting with Row 1, Unit I (see Figure 12).

Figure 12: Row 1, Unit I.

UNIT I	Learn to define achievement	Draw self achieving	Learn about ACT	Learn to work in a group	Set goals and strive in a game	Learn the six achievement steps

Unit I: Introduction to the instructional program. Think of the cells in this first row as a general guide for introducing the concepts, ideas, and information that your learners will need to start using the strategy. With these lessons you are setting the foundation for cognitive verbal processing. There is no mystery here, since this is pretty much what any instructor would do in any instructional setting.

Unit I, Cell 1 introduces the strategy's basic terms: vocabulary, such *as internal control, achievement, striving,* and *goals,* and presents the logic behind the idea that to control our lives we must act to achieve, and that in order to achieve we must set goals and strive to achieve them.

The aim of the lesson presented in Unit I, Cell 2 aims to help the learner objectify himself, to see himself as achieving from a third-person point of view. We ask the learners to think of examples from their own lives and then share and discuss their examples. We also explore some illustrations from the lives of others, perhaps those of prominent figures. Having appropriate examples from the domain area of your focus, such as vocational, sports, or health achievements, is always useful.

Unit I, Cell 3 focuses on informing the learners about the organization of the training course. This explanation includes an overview of expectations and activities. For example, as mentioned earlier, one of the most effective and useful activities is journaling, where learners write down their thoughts and record their activities throughout their participation in the course. Take the time to answer questions like "Will there be tests?" "Will we be required to write?"

This is also a good time to discuss time expectations, how to make up any lost work, and so on. Naturally, you will design your own process and procedures that will be appropriate to your situation.

Unit I, Cell 4 addresses how learners work together. For this purpose, we have created a programmed training exercise that teaches learners ways to work effectively in groups. This is a very important aspect of the instructional program because learners will often be called upon to work in groups around sharing ideas, reacting to the ideas of others, and working together on a task. With our fifth graders it helped to put a list of six rules together for them to observe when they were participating in a group task. This group process training turned out to be very effective.

The written directions that guided our fifth graders can be seen in Figures 13A and 13B (on the next page). Many of the teachers in our classroom program remarked on how well the children were able to work together in groups after this training and how this positive group behavior carried over into other class activities. This technique may or may not be appropriate for your situation, but if you do expect to employ group processes in your instructional program, I strongly recommend that you take the time to train your learners in group behavior. It will pay off.

Figure 13A: Rules for working in a group.

The first unit introduces and teaches the students the vocabulary, concepts and procedures they will need to effectively participate in the rest of the package. For instance, Unit I teaches rules for working in groups that will enable the students to function more effectively when working with each other during the lessons. Here are six rules that the children learn and practice.

This lesson divides the class into two groups. While one group discusses a problem, the other monitors with the following score card.

Unit 1, Cell 5 introduces a fun game called Achievo that engages learners in utilizing the vocabulary and concepts of the strategy. This game is probably not appropriate for adults. With that said, it could be upgraded and adapted if you felt you would have the chance to use if often.

Figure 13B: Rules for working in a group.

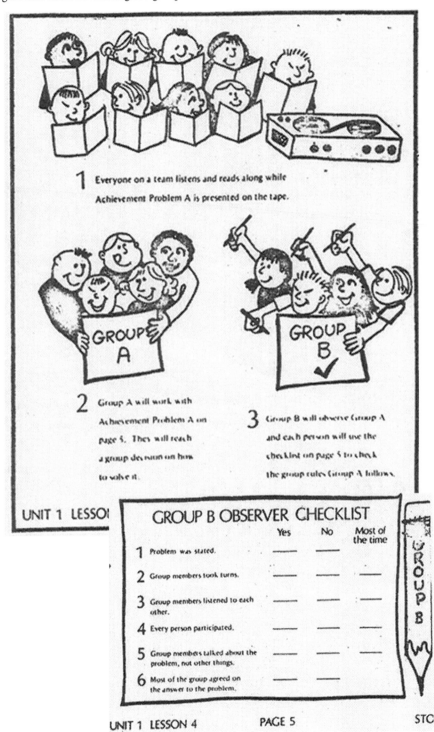

1 Everyone on a team listens and reads along while Achievement Problem A is presented on the tape.

2 Group A will work with Achievement Problem A on page 5. They will reach a group decision on how to solve it.

3 Group B will observe Group A and each person will use the checklist on page 5 to check the group rules Group A follows.

UNIT 1 LESSON

GROUP B OBSERVER CHECKLIST

		Yes	No	Most of the time
1	Problem was stated.	___	___	___
2	Group members took turns.	___	___	___
3	Group members listened to each other.	___	___	___
4	Every person participated.	___	___	___
5	Group members talked about the problem, not other things.	___	___	___
6	Most of the group agreed on the answer to the problem.	___	___	___

GROUP B

UNIT 1 LESSON 4   PAGE 5   STO

Unit I, Cell 6 focuses on hammering home the words and concepts of the strategy. The objective is for learners to be able to name the steps and recognize them in action. This is a straight-out drill, practice, and learn-it activity. Presumably, once they've reached this point, learners will be prepared to begin learning to use the strategy step by step.

Let's take another look at the curriculum layout. Note that the names of the strategy steps are listed across the top of the six cells in the second row with each cell having a label above it. Each cell below these labels focuses on the one strategy step labeled above it. As learners proceed through the six cells, they learn about and execute the step that is labeled above until they arrive at the final step, "evaluate." They then repeat this process in the third row, learning more about each step and executing the strategy through to a second complete round. Hence, they actually begin using the strategy in Unit II.

Figure 14: Unit II (Strategy Step 1).

UNIT II	Name past achievements	Get goal ideas from past achievements	Make goal specific	Name and order tasks	Use envisioning achievement and heroes	Decide how well you did

Unit II, Cell 1 (Strategy Step 1): Study Self. In this strategy step we ask the learners to name their past achievements. Absolutely no discussion or reference to problems, needs, failures, or weaknesses is allowed. No, never! Remember, people can easily name things they feel they need to improve, along with their failings and weaknesses, but tend to sputter and hesitate when asked to name past achievements and strengths. It helps to always bear in mind that we need to build on past achievements and strengths for energy and inspiration.

Several ideas are at work here. First, we want to ignite and fan a positive attitude—that good feeling that emanates from successful achievement. Second, we want to get learners to think of themselves as effective, successful, and purposeful *doers*. Third, we want learners to articulate and acknowledge these achievements, and have them recognized and certified by others. Fourth, we want learners to use this information about themselves as the sources for new goal ideas for their future actions and as inspiration to achieve.

This step is important because we want learners to adopt the perspective that they are successful achievers. We want them to look at themselves objectively and to begin to build a bank of self-perceptions that are reinforcing and supportive of their power to act successfully.

This is the internal stuff of internal control: a documentation of their uniqueness, of who they are, who they want to be, and what they want to do.

The fundamental activity in this cell is list making. First, you will need to discuss what is meant by "past achievements" and offer some examples to further your learners' understanding. Seat the learners individually with a blank piece of paper in front of each one. Ask them to list their past achievements, giving them a four- or five-minute period of silence in which to make their lists. Then ask them to share their first examples. Discuss and expand on these examples. Lead with some challenging questions such as, "Can you think of an achievement that only you think is an achievement, but it's still important to you because it was a breakthrough?" Have some examples at hand to expand the learners' idea of what might be included, such as, "I overcame my fear of public speaking enough to make a class report, even though I was scared to death...frozen. But I did it." Using examples from different domains that you want to make sure are covered is helpful. For example, if you are working with diabetic patients, examples related to achievements of other individuals who are diabetic will be more meaningful.

It is also important to be mindful of building an accepting climate as you go so that learners will reinforce each other's input. With our fifth graders we used some helpful gimmicks, such as check lists. You can shape the content of these check lists to focus on the kind and quality of the responses you want. This helps expand the learners' ideas and responses. As mentioned earlier, in the Internal Control Program we used the symbol of a mirror to represent self-study and actually provided aluminum foil mirrors for the children to use to study themselves. We then had the children list their past achievements and strengths on the border of the mirror. This is just one way to ensure your learners are having fun as they learn.

The result we want from this first step of the strategy is a list of personal past achievements for each learner. We want the learners to value these achievements and keep them foremost in their minds. This is positive and enabling stuff! It is the self-perspective we want them to have. For this reason, one of our gimmicky activities was to have the children create a list that they could keep and frame. We referred to this list as their Bank of Achievement, and suggested that they hang the list on a wall in their room so it would be there for inspiration. Here is an example of a couple of Banks of Achievement (see Figures15A and 15B).

Figure 15A: Bank of Achievement reflects personal past achievements.

Figure 15B: Bank of Achievement reflects personal past achievements.

We have suggested five domains of achievements here, but you can (and probably should) suggest domain areas appropriate to your purposes and for your learners. For example, if you are a sales manager working with your marketing team or a therapist working with a disabled client, you will want to list topics or domains appropriate to your intent and objectives.

We also suggest that you have your learners create a list of past achievements appropriate for keeping in their records. You might even bring some picture frames to your instructional group for permanent framing. The idea that your learners are and have been achievers—goal-getters and go-getters—is that important. Creating a personal meaningful definition of achievement becomes an energy springboard for every single learner.

There is even a dividend for you, the instructor, as you proceed.

You now have some very special and personal information about each of your learners. You have forged a bond. You have a bridge of communication that grants you influence with each individual learner. In the future you can use this information to relate to the learner in a personalized and significant manner. If you are a parent working with a child, for example, the information you discover will help you encourage and support him in his endeavors by referring to his past achievements and strengths.

The same is true if you are a teacher, supervisor, or friend. In all cases you can be a supporter and energizer, as well as a much more effective guide and teacher. You will also find that this personal bond grows as you and your learners move through the steps of the strategy, a consequence that is very rewarding for you, the instructor. You will feel good in a deep and personal way.

. . .

Now that we have our list of strengths, we are ready to go on to the next step of the strategy: Get Goal Ideas (see Figures 16 and 17).

Figure 16: Unit II.

UNIT II	Name past achievements	Get goal ideas from past achievements	Make goal specific	Name and order tasks	Use envisioning achievement and heroes	Decide how well you did

Unit II, Cell 2 (Strategy Step 2): Get Goal Ideas. In this strategy step we ask learners to brainstorm goal ideas by utilizing the information from the first step of the strategy. We ask them to generate ideas of things they would like to achieve based on their lists of past achievements. The end product of this strategy step is a list of goal ideas that can become the basis for the careful formulation of an actual goal in the next step of the strategy.

The basic method employed is that of classic brainstorming or "divergent thinking." First, review the rules of brainstorming with your learners. Emphasize that when brainstorming anything goes. Let them know that you will jot everything down, and that you'd like them to generate thoughts, be fast, and get goofy if they want. Show them that there is no judgment; that you will be putting down whatever you hear, whether it seems "reasonable" or not. Finally, if you are working with a group, have the learners work individually first and then brainstorm as a group. (Check the literature on brainstorming for additional ideas and tips.)

Figure 17: Lesson 2: Getting goal Ideas from past achievements.

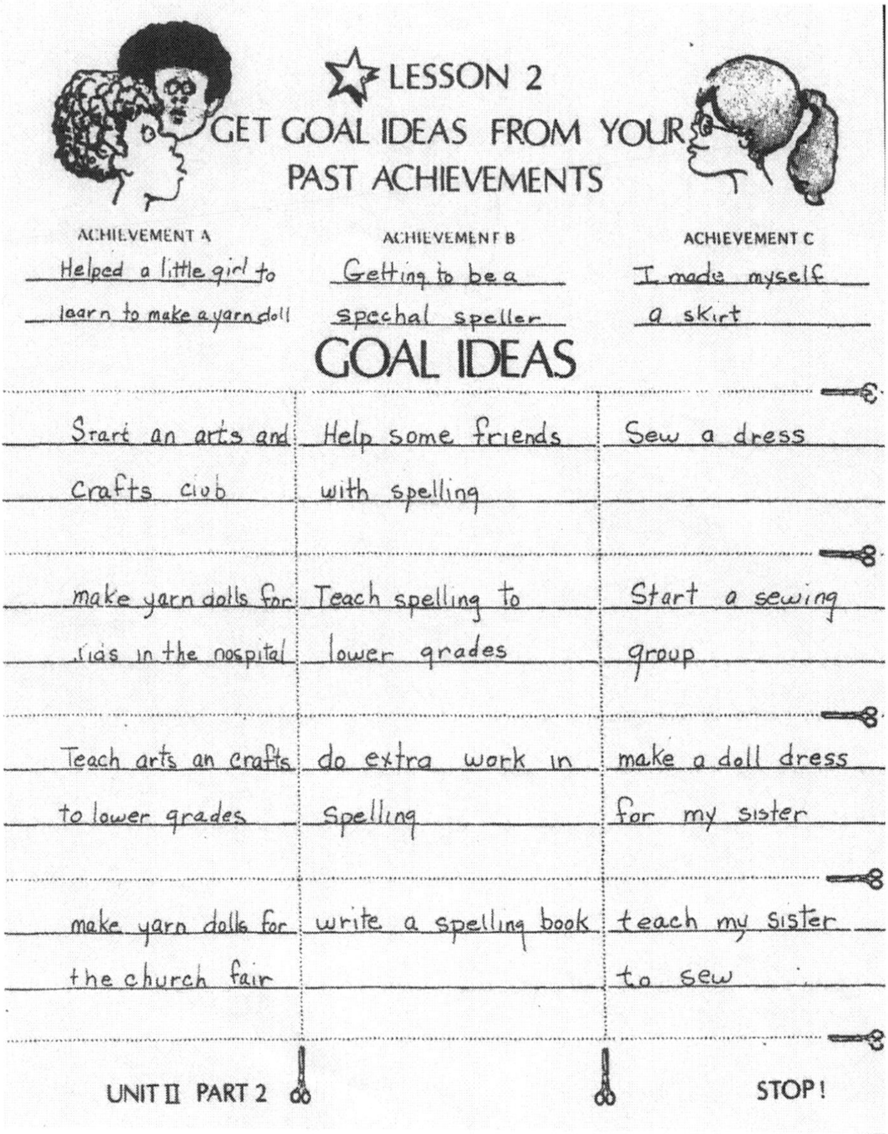

★ LESSON 2
GET GOAL IDEAS FROM YOUR PAST ACHIEVEMENTS

ACHIEVEMENT A	ACHIEVEMENT B	ACHIEVEMENT C
Helped a little girl to learn to make a yarn doll	Getting to be a spechal speller	I made myself a skirt

GOAL IDEAS

Srart an arts and crafts ciub	Help some friends with spelling	Sew a dress
make yarn dolls for rids in the nospital	Teach spelling to lower grades	Start a sewing group
Teach arts an crafts to lower grades	do extra work in Spelling	make a doll dress for my sister
make yarn dolls for the church fair	write a spelling book	teach my sister to sew

UNIT II PART 2 ✂   ✂   STOP!

There are two additional things you should try to accomplish in addition to producing a list of goal ideas. First, drive the learners to expand their goal ideas beyond what they think are the expectations of others. As we were developing this strategy we found that the children initially came up with ideas that they thought would please the researchers, their teachers, and their parents. This is the initial response of many individuals, especially Externals, who respond with what they believe to be expected by others. They are not looking at their past achievements or at their strengths, but at their idea of what they assume other people want from them. You must work to break their gaze from a focus outside themselves and help them focus on their own personal past successes and strengths. This is one of the key aspects of moving from being an External toward becoming an Internal. By encouraging your learners to "focus on what you want to do" and to "do your own thing" whenever you have the opportunity, you will guide them in this process.

Second, we want the learners to perceive themselves as individuals who can accomplish what they set out to do as actors or agents for their own lives. We want them to practice looking at the world as doers who do things that they want to do, and who can act to further their past accomplishments and build on their strengths. Brainstorming goal ideas requires them to imagine things that they want to do and to take control of their lives and invest in moving toward their goals. This is an important rehearsal for the consistent exercise of internal control. We are teaching learners what it means and how it feels to act by "building on past achievements and strengths." I urge you to articulate these thoughts and explain this thinking at every opportunity. Don't keep the meaning and reasons for your actions to yourself. Hammer home these ideas that are inherent in internal control.

Unit II, Cell 3 (Strategy Step 3): Set a Goal. In this strategy step we ask the learners to name and commit to a goal that is both doable and short term and specific in number, time, and kind. This involves learning some skills, which require detailed instruction, drill, and practice. For that reason, there is some serious convergent thinking needed here. This requires a change in tone: the learners have to put their noses down and learn.

Remember that goal setting is a key control point because it sets the stage for the learner's success or failure. Setting a goal that is not actually doable dooms the learner's effort to meaninglessness and even ridicule. Again, "To grow to be a 7-foot NBA basketball star" is not doable. "To practice to be able to make 5 out of 10 foul shots within a month" *is* doable. Teaching this concept of "do-ability" will vary with the intelligence and maturity of your learners. Fifth graders needed some guidance with examples of doable goals and help in rewriting their own non-doable goals into doable ones. Though you won't need as much drill on this skill when working with educated adults, the point still must be made and listed as a criteria for goal formulation.

We must also help learners set goals that are specific. Without specificity learners cannot know if and when they have achieved their goals. Specifically defining goals increases focus and commitment on the part of the learner. "I am going to make some cookies" initially sounds okay as a goal. But it's so vague that we have to wonder if we'll ever see those cookies. Teach the learners to practice making their goals specific by including relevant details, such as time, kind, number, and medium risk. "I am going to make two dozen chocolate chip cookies this coming Saturday morning," for example, is a specific goal. Do we think we have a chance of seeing these cookies made? Do we feel the in commitment in this goal statement?

Here are some examples of the exercises we used with our fifth-grade learners (see Figure 18):

Figure 18: Step 3: Setting a Goal.

PRACTICE

DIRECTIONS:
● FIND THE KIND, QUANTITY AND TIME IN EACH GOAL STATEMENT.
● WRITE EACH BOUNDARY ON THE LINES UNDER THE STATEMENT.

PRACTICE EXAMPLE

GOAL STATEMENT:

Do 2 pages of math by tomorrow.

Kind: _____

Quantity: _____

Time: _____

1 GOAL STATEMENT:

Collect 10 baseball cards by next Thursday.

Kind: _____

Quantity: _____

Time: _____

UNIT II LESSON 3   PAGE 3

☆ **PART 3**

DIRECTIONS:

1 WRITE 3 GOAL IDEAS FROM LESSON 2

2 MAKE THE IDEA SPECIFIC. WRITE THE

...KIND · WHAT IS THE COLOR OR SIZE OR TYPE OF THING?

...QUANTITY · HOW MUCH OR HOW MANY?

...TIME · HOW LONG WILL IT TAKE?

3 WRITE THE SPECIFIC GOAL STATEMENT

MY OWN GOALS

1 Goal idea: _____

Kind: _____

Quantity: _____

Time: _____

Goal Statement: _____
_____

UNIT II LESSON 3   PAGE 8   GO ON ▶

As our fifth graders approached the end of working with this strategy step they were required to formulate a goal that they wanted to achieve. Most importantly, this goal they would "set" would be one that they would commit to achieve. The learners then shared their goals with the others in the group and made a commitment to achieve their goal. This was an exciting and climatic experience for the learners (see Figure 19)!

Figure 19: My Own Goals: Setting goals and committing to achieve them.

Unit II, Cell 4 (Strategy Step 4): Plan. Now that the learners have set a specific and doable goal, the next step is to plan. Internals are process-conscious. They know how to plan and how to ask nuts-and-bolts questions. They are concerned with *how* a task is to be implemented. They know how to plan and they do plan. Our objective is to encourage learners to name and order the tasks required to achieve a specific goal—in other words, to plan.

In talking about planning we make an assumption that though most people already know how to plan, many do not. For example, most people are capable of setting a budget for themselves, but do not; instead they act on impulse with only a vague idea of the larger consequences. That is why learners have to be sold on the need to plan. To this end, we strongly suggest that you start out addressing the question of why planning is important by talking about the value and need for planning. Presenting case studies of people who did not plan and the consequences of their not planning can further this objective.

In essence, we want our learners to know that planning pays! That it is the smart, internal thing to do. Arm yourself with some anecdotes from your own experience that are appropriate to your objectives and to your learner group. Induce your learners to offer examples from their own experiences. Sell the idea of planning and convince your learners to invest in planning. Combined, this adds up to more than half the task of teaching the planning step.

From this point on we can focus on learners' naming and ordering tasks to achieve specific goals. Providing examples of goals that are appropriate for your learners and having learners individually list tasks for specific goals and share them with others creates a healthy learning situation where learners are working together to brainstorm tasks. I have found that this process makes learners excited about working toward their goals. They are ready to get to work, to strive!

It is at this point that we introduce the Achievement Worksheet, which becomes the learner's plan (see Figure 20).

Figure 20: Achievement Worksheet: the Learner's Plan.

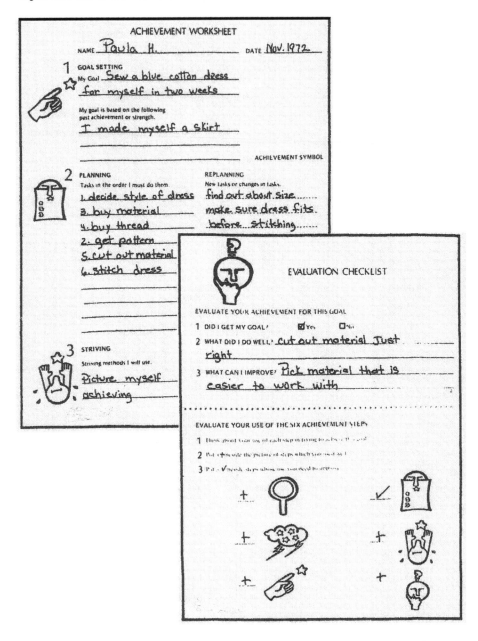

Unit II, Cell 5 (Strategy Step 5): Strive. This step introduces the idea that we have to work to get our goals, and have to work our plans to make our goals happen. This step introduces an idea that is not widely accepted in our society, namely that an individual is responsible for managing his striving, his moods, and his motivation; that we should not be victims of our feelings and our moods. The message is this: If you are not in the mood to work, if you don't feel motivated...all you have to do is change the way you feel! You are responsible if you do or if you don't. You *can* change your mood...and here is how you can do it.

Again, we began by highlighting the problem that occurs when learners have a goal, but are having difficulty striving or working to achieve that goal. We model a case situation to focus on this common human experience. You can describe an example to your learners and then ask them to share some of their own experiences. We took our fifth graders on two "guided meditation" trips, one into the past and one into the future, and had them experience two striving methods: remembering past achievements and picturing successful achievement.

In a second lesson the children worked in groups to remember heroes or people that they admired and then wrote down their positive attributes. Then we discussed how thinking about heroes can inspire us and how their stories can help us strive to reach our own goals.

In a subsequent lesson we presented three case studies and asked the children to identify the striving methods that were being used. We asked them to try to discover their own personal striving styles by reviewing a list of striving methods and checking off those that they have or might use. They were encouraged to include any personal striving methods they employed, such as "talking to Mom" or "making work a game." To conclude, we had the children choose one or more striving method to use as they continued to work on their currently selected goal and to write it down on their on their Achievement Worksheet.

The objectives of this lesson are to:

1. Introduce the idea that we can manage and are responsible for managing our own striving;
2. Help learners become aware that there are specific techniques that they can use and already use effectively to manage their striving;
3. Help learners develop a personal style of managing their striving; and
4. Help learners select and use at least one striving method to work toward achieving a personal goal.

Unit II, Cell 6 (Strategy Step 6): Evaluate. The function of this lesson is to introduce the idea that it is worthwhile to make an effort to evaluate your efforts. Internals are very interested in the results of their efforts. They want to know what they did well and what they did wrong. They want this information in order to improve their performance, in order to improve their control of their effectiveness. They want details and they seek criticism.

That is why we focus on legitimizing the importance of evaluating one's efforts. We offer learners the chance to practice evaluating their personal achievement efforts. Appropriate case studies also offer learners the opportunity for evaluation.

The objectives of this cell are to teach learners that:

1. Thoughtful evaluation is an important internal control behavior;
2. Evaluating personal achievement can be done by assessing whether the goal was achieved; and
3. Evaluating one's actions by stating in detail what was done well and what could be improved is beneficial.

This concludes our discussion of the content of the Unit II row and one round where our learners have used the strategy to achieve a personal goal.

. . .

Unit I develops concepts and vocabulary. Unit II teaches the initial skills of the Personal Achievement Strategy. Now, Unit III expands on the skills and concepts of the previous units and continues to emphasize the active use of the six steps to attain goals (see Figure 21). For example, the concept of specificity is reviewed in Cell III-2 and then extended in III-3 to the concept of "medium risk" so learners can appreciate that being able to state a goal in specific terms can help them make the goal medium risk as well. In Cell III-4, practice in "re-planning" builds on the planning experience gained in Unit II. In Cell III-5, learners are introduced to the use of three kinds of competition that they can add to their repertoire of striving methods. In effect, we are building on the past units, reviewing them, and introducing new, but related, concepts and skills.

Figure 21: Unit III.

	Name personal strengths	Get goal ideas from strengths	Make goal medium risk	Replan when faced with problems	Use competition	Evaluate progress with ACT
UNIT III						

Unit III, Cell 1 (Step 1): Study Self. In this cell we introduce the idea of identifying and naming strengths. This builds upon the previous skill of naming past achievements and is done the same way and for the same reason: because it's energizing. Naming strengths builds confidence and a positive outlook. Naming strengths creates a feeling of empowerment and reinforces the idea that the learner has power and can be an effective participant in the world. These strengths also become the source for new goal ideas.

Naming strengths can be a real high for learners. They feel good and are ready to engage in a number of activities. If the members know each other, as the fifth graders did, it's a good opportunity for them to share "strength suggestions." We had the children send each other "Strength-o-grams." Wow! What a powerful experience it is to have someone else tell you that you have a strength and share with you exactly what it is. The children loved it (see Figure 22).

Figure 22: Strength-o-gram.

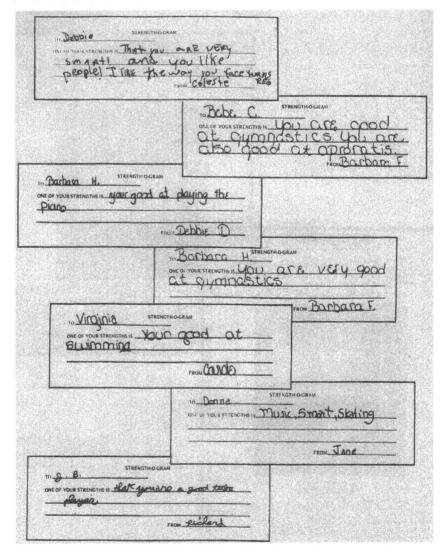

Some of the things you can do include adapting or constructing that valuable tool, the check list, to introduce and enlarge the learners' understanding of what "strengths" are, e.g., loyalty, honesty, and so on. You can also introduce ideas about strengths that are germane to your learners. For example, if you are working with athletes you can add strengths that relate to maintaining workout schedules.

Encouraging your learners to keep their lists of strengths in some permanent form and to review them from time is always helpful. Like their list of past achievements, the list of strengths can and will be a source of confidence and inspiration in the future.

Unit III, Cell 2 (Step 2): Get Goal Ideas. This step is very similar to the exercise of using past achievements to generate goal ideas. We used these exercises to review and employ the rule for making the goals doable and specific in kind, number, and time. The end result of these activities was a list of specific goal ideas.

Unit III, Cell 3 (Step 3): Set a Goal. This cell focuses on selecting a goal and learning the importance and skill of making goals medium risk. Setting a goal at too high a risk level, at too difficult a level, will probably end in failure. As we know, Externals consistently set goals that are either too high or too low. Internals are careful to commit to goals that are probably attainable, and control their lives by setting goals of this nature. They often lower their goals to have less risk and set more modest objectives when they fail or fall short. This is an extremely important concept. Spend time on it. It's something that clearly distinguishes Externals from Internals. The ideal is to set a goal that a individual has a 60% probability of attaining. This will be a goal that is challenging, but not difficult enough that it will be improbable to reach.

It is worth mentioning the topic of procrastination in this context. One theory holds that when we seek to carry out a task that is too ambiguous either in quality or quantity, we are inhibited by its perceived difficulty. It works like this: I am a widower and I am living in a medium-sized house. Periodically I realize that the house needs a good cleaning. However, I procrastinate because it is a big job. I would have to stop everything I'm doing and just clean. I put it off. Then I realize that my goal of cleaning the entire house is too much. So now I lower my goal and determine to clean only the two bathrooms by Thursday. It works. I do it. Then I set another small goal, to clean two of the bedrooms. That works, too, and so I proceed by taking small steps. Internals maintain momentum and get things done by having medium-risk and smaller, more easily attainable goals.

This contradicts popular culture's call to set high goals and avoid aiming too low. We're told that those with lofty goals are going "to be somebody." But the literature predicts that individuals who set too-high goals generally will not be successful. Teach that there is no need to be either the tortoise or the hare, that setting modest, attainable goals helps us become successful achievers.

. . .

We started this lesson with the ring toss, a game somewhat like quoits. This game is well documented in the literature and is used to study risk-level styles. In this game, learners predict their scores and try to do their best to attain a good score. There are several rounds. The learners can set and adjust different levels of risk as they proceed through the game. The experience is quite revealing for all. Parents are typically impressed with how they begin to see the individual risk styles of their children, as are the children when seeing their parents play the game. I recommend that you use this game. It has also been successfully used with many adults who find it revealing and instructive. The game session concludes with a discussion of risk levels.

The lessons in this cell continue to develop the value of setting medium-risk goals. Learners practice identifying risk levels and rewriting goal statements to make them medium risk (see Figure 23).

Figure 23: Is Your Goal Medium Risk?

This lesson concludes by having the learners rewrite their selected goal level and discuss it with others to see if they think the goal is now medium risk. Evidence shows that we were quite successful in teaching this concept and its related skills (see Figure 24).

Figure 24: Setting medium-risk goals.

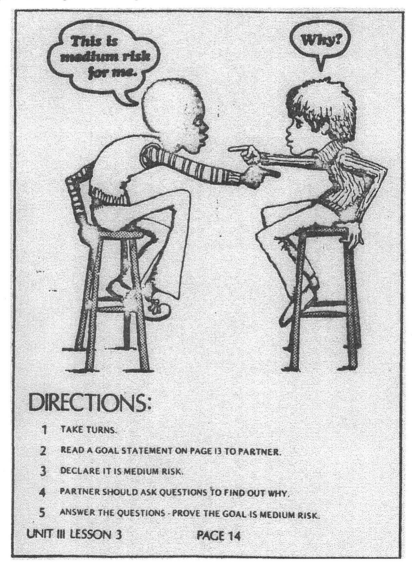

The objectives of this cell are to:

1. Identify the risk level of goal statements;
2. Rewrite goal statements judged to be high or low risk as medium-risk statements;
3. Recall that successful achievers set medium-risk goals;
4. Demonstrate understanding of medium risk by explaining why a personal goal is medium risk; and
5. Set a goal personally judged to be specific and medium risk.

Unit III, Cell 4 (Step 4): Plan. The main objective of this cell is to teach the learner to question and seek information about planning and re-planning as necessary. We all know that even when we make a plan and start to work it we can count on unanticipated events to occur. We have to be flexible, and even aggressively flexible. This means expecting change, seeking information about the possibility of needed change, and expecting to adjust our plans or to re-plan. The Internal does this willingly; the External tends to be inflexible and rigid.

This lesson begins with a review of planning. Learners work individually to name and order the task required to achieve their self-selected goals, then work in pairs to review each others' plans. Following this activity, learners are presented with some cases where goals were set and plans were made that then needed to be changed. Our fifth graders were given experience in re-planning by having them take an imaginary trip down a river in South America. Working with a map in their journals, they were periodically given new information about their situation. Each time, they were asked to remark their intended route in a different color if they thought it was necessary. ("Look out for those falls ahead!") We suggest that you develop a similar simulation appropriate to your learners and topic area.

In the next lesson learners work in pairs. The lesson opens with "Slice of Life" episodes that introduce the idea of questioning plans and seeking information about plans after they are made. Learners role play Slice of Life characters and try to devise questions about their plans. Then learners are asked to question their own plans and to re-plan as necessary on their Achievement Worksheets.

The objective for this cell is to learn to question and seek information about a plan and to re-plan as necessary.

UNIT III, Cell 5 (Step 5): Strive. The general function of this lesson is to teach the use of three kinds of competition as methods for striving: competition with self, competition with others, and competition with a standard of excellence. Though differing opinions about the efficacy of using competition in our society exist, there is clear agreement that competition generates ENERGY and the motivation to strive. This is illustrated in examples ranging from spelling bees to high school sports to corporate sales contests. The goal is to teach that manipulation does not have to come from an external source; instead, we can profitably "manipulate" our own circumstances. One way to do this is through competition. Competition is a powerful tool for generating learner's enthusiasm and energy. Use it.

Situations and case studies are provided so learners can experience each kind of competition and to illustrate how individuals can use these kinds of competition to help them strive. The learners are asked to employ some form of competition to help them strive for the goal that they have set, and then to add their findings to their Achievement Worksheet, as below (see Figures 25A and B).

Figure 25A: Compete with Excellence activity.

DIRECTIONS:

1 PICK SOMEONE TO COMPETE WITH.

2 WRITE THIS PERSON'S NAME ON THE LINE BELOW.

_____

3 TAKE TURNS JUMPING.

4 COUNT THE NUMBER OF JUMPS YOU MAKE IN ONE HALF MINUTE.

5 RETURN TO YOUR DESKS.

Write your number here ☐

Write the other person's score here ☐

STOP - turn the tape on

1 How did you do?

☐ won   ☐ lost   ☐ tied

2 Did competing with another help you strive?

☐ very much   ☐ somewhat   ☐ not very much   ☐ not at all

3 Do you think you can learn to use competition with others to help you strive?

☐ yes   ☐ no   ☐ maybe

Figure 25B: Compete with Excellence activity.

☆ PART 3

Compete with excellence

THINK OF THE HIGHEST NUMBER OF JUMPS YOU THINK YOU CAN POSSIBLY MAKE IN HALF A MINUTE. WRITE THE NUMBER IN THE BOX TITLED "MY STANDARD OF EXCELLENCE."

MY STANDARD OF EXCELLENCE

DIRECTIONS:

1 JUMP AS BEFORE.

2 COUNT THE NUMBER OF JUMPS AS BEFORE AND WRITE IT IN THE BOX TITLED "MY ACTUAL SCORE."

MY ACTUAL SCORE

3 WHEN YOU ARE FINISHED, RETURN TO YOUR DESKS AND TURN THE TAPE ON.

ANSWER THESE QUESTIONS AFTER THE EXPERIMENT

1 How did you do in comparison to your standard of excellence?

☐ better   ☐ as well   ☐ not good   ☐ not even near

2 Did competing with a standard of excellence help you strive harder?

☐ yes   ☐ no   ☐ maybe

3 Do you think you could learn to use competition with a standard of excellence to help you strive?

☐ yes   ☐ no   ☐ maybe

UNIT III LESSON 5   PAGE 9   STOP!

This lesson's objectives are to identify the three kinds of competitive striving and to indicate ways to use competition in personal striving.

UNIT III; Cell 6 (Step 6): Evaluation. The general function of this lesson is to provide opportunities for learners to evaluate themselves as achievers. Whereas previously learners focused on their success in achieving goals and evaluating/deciding what they did well and what could use improvement, now they are asked to evaluate their use of the strategy itself. How can they improve their use of the Personal Achievement Strategy? First they evaluate examples and then their own use of the strategy using their Achievement Worksheet. Then, as the concluding step in this part of the process (Unit III), they report on their success in achieving their personal goals. (Please refer to any of the Achievement Worksheets provided above).

UNIT IV, Cells 1 through 6 (see Figure 26).

Figure 26: UNIT IV.

UNIT III	Name personal strengths	Get goal ideas from strengths	Make goal medium risk	Replan when faced with problems	Use competition	Evaluate progress with ACT

Unit IV differs from the other units in that the learners engage in achievement efforts as a group in pursuit of a class goal. Following the pattern established in Units II and II, the class studies itself relative to its past achievements and strengths and then brainstorms new class goals, sets a class goal, and plans and strives as a group. This acts as a third use of the strategy and reinforces its use as the learners discuss and use the strategy steps.

This approach works extremely well, resulting in very positive projects (see reports and teachers' comments discussed in Chapter 4). If you have the opportunity to have your learners work in a group after they have learned the strategy, I urge you to do so. The process is fun, the results can be amazing and confirming, and you will build morale and a sense of empowerment and responsibility in your group.

Summary

In conclusion, I hope that the detailed information on using the Personal Achievement Strategy instructional formats provided in this chapter will help you to create an instructional program appropriate for your own unique learner group and situation.

More specific accounts of this instructional program are available for purchase at teachinternalcontrol. com. These more detailed accounts can be found in the *ACT Teacher's Manual: Achievement Competence Training* and the *ACT Student Journal: Achievement Competence Training Journal*.

Chapter 8

Check List of Principles, Procedures, and Activities for Teaching the Personal Achievement Strategy

This is a check list of ideas, concepts, and suggested approaches that you might consider as you begin to teach internal locus of control. As before, I suggest that you might make a list for you occasional referral. I hope these suggestions, formed over the last 40 years of my teaching internality, will be helpful to you as you teach internal locus of control.

1. Address learners as agents, as deciders, not as minions or order-takers. If you do decide to go into a "top sergeant" mode, try to give reasons for doing it. "Now we need to learn the symbols for these chemical elements so we can understand what comes next. So, let's not play around; learn them, memorize them. Do it."

2. Shift responsibility to the learners of the activity by having them set goals, plans, and so on. Engaging them in decisions about the process is a sure way to make this happen.

3. Create leeway for real decision making. There must be a sense on the part of learners that they have some control—a measure of freedom for them to decide what goals they wish to set and how much they want to achieve and at what level. Encouraging them to participate in selecting planning and striving options will ensure their ongoing decision making efforts.

4. Use visuals. Put a poster depicting the strategy steps on the wall. Have learners make posters of their own depicting the individual step of making goals specific and medium risk. Put up slogans to bolster confidence and retention.

5. Model all the internal control steps that you employ in your teaching. Verbalize them. For example, share your objectives for the class when teaching different lessons. Sharing your own thinking out loud when you evaluate an activity and communicating what it is that you are doing will help make the strategy more accessible to the learners and help them understand how to apply it.

6. Encourage (or even require) journaling. Writing in a journal about one's personal thoughts and feelings is a powerful mechanism for developing internal control, one supported by the research.[5] Learners who record their past achievements, strengths, and interests or who write about using the strategy steps (from new goal ideas to goal setting to evaluating themselves and deciding what they want to do better), will find they have learned a great life habit!

7. Encourage and allow "process talk." "Do any of you have trouble getting yourself to do your homework? Well, I guess this is a pretty common problem, right? Does anyone have ways that they use to get going and get it done? Great. …Mary, you have your hand up, tell us what works for you." Be accepting of the learners' feelings and ideas about their personal challenges and successes.

8. Use the information that you gain from your learners' use of the strategy to help and reinforce their behaviors. "Okay, John, how's it going with your plan to earn money for a new computer? Any progress? How much have you saved?" … "Bobby how are you doing in your effort to improve your math grade. Any success?"

9. Develop group skills so learners can work together effectively to reinforce and experience group achievement and control. Consider teaching the six rules of group work that were taught as part of the Internal Control Program. (You can refer to the literature for many such programs of instruction.) Get the whole group working together.

10. Emphasize striving and work over talent. "Rachel, I see you're doing very well in math. I know you've been putting in the work and it shows." This is a good chance to share success with the rest of the group. "The rest of you can learn from Rachel—that doing well requires effort." Don't allow learners to excuse themselves "because they don't have any talent" or it's "not their thing." (An interesting note: Some researchers tell us that one thing that may account for Japanese learners doing better in math is because the Japanese learners believe that doing well in math is a function of effort and work—that if you work harder you will do better, whereas many American learners believe that doing well in math is a function of talent, where you either have it or you don't. If this is functionally true, that many Americans don't do well in math because they believe they just don't have the talent, it might also mean that they may stop making an effort and end up doing worse than they might otherwise if their belief system were different.) Kill this attitude. Fight it at all times. It is disabling.

11. Promote medium-risk goal setting. It is smart to set goals that are fairly easy, but not too easy, to achieve. Big or difficult goals or grand-sounding goals make it hard to even start striving. Too-difficult goals make it probable for us to fail and perhaps give up. It's okay to have big long-range goals, but important to break them down into smaller steps. Let's take the eighth-grader who decides she wants to be a medical doctor. That's great! But right now she needs to begin to think about the steps in between, such as getting a good grade on the next science test. Help your learners understand that great journeys are composed of many small steps. This is a very important concept to communicate. Also help them understand that lowering the difficulty or amount of a goal can help them overcome procrastination and get started.

12. Use contracts. If you are comfortable, sit down and talk with your learners about what they are going to try to do. This requires that you discuss goal possibilities and set a specific goal. Sound familiar? "Contracting" gives you the opportunity to work on planning with the learner, and later to have an opportunity to evaluate their efforts with them. That *is* the Personal Achievement Strategy. Teachers use contracts, parents use contracts, and supervisors use contracts. Their use can benefit everyone.

13. Take the time to have learners experience the good feeling associated with past achievements and more recent achievements—and celebrate as appropriate. Actually taking time out to have your learners think about their achievements as well as sharing their achievements and their related feelings with an accepting group can be extremely rewarding. You might make these sessions wide open to topics or you might focus on certain activities, such as math class or on-the-job employment tasks. Rather than always being the praise-giver yourself, try shifting the responsibility to the learners. Providing the opportunity for them to report their achievements will induce them to express themselves and feel positively about that expression.

14. Develop an Achievement Worksheet tailored to your enterprise. The worksheet should include the internal strategy steps with the sub-rules as check-offs. Some steps may be de-emphasized because they don't apply or they might be stated a little differently due to the nature of your enterprise. An English teacher might develop one for theme writing; a sales manager might develop one for weekly or monthly planning and goal setting. Achievement Worksheets can then be easily converted into a contract after being reviewed by all concerned. Be careful not to use a worksheet as a coercive devise to control your learners or employees! This is *their* worksheet. It is for them, and for what they plan to do. They may consult with you for advice and help, but they must control the content. Otherwise this becomes your thing, not theirs.

15. Encourage the use of to-do lists by all the learners. As we know, Internals tend to use to-do lists, specifically because they are valuable tools for focusing and controlling daily actions and getting results. To-do lists are best used in the context of goals that have been set by the user, but again, they should not at any time become a method for you or anyone else to control the user. Instead they are for the user and for you in aiding the user to achieve his goals. If you are a parent or manager you can promote the use of daily to-do lists based on the fact that regular list-making develops a sense of internal control. (Refer to the literature on "time management" for many additional ideas and examples.)

16. Encourage self-evaluation. The first reason for encouraging self-evaluation is to be sure that learners take credit for what they do well. Feel it and enjoy it with them. Have them remember this part of their evaluation. Don't skip over it and focus on the anxiety-producing negatives, as is the tendency for many of us. Foster the learner's ability to savor and enjoy his successful achievements. The second reason to encourage self-evaluation is that it provides an opportunity for identifying what the learner can do to improve. This does not mean focusing on the negative outcome! Our goal is to leave the learner with a positive focus, the sense of, "I can improve and will try to improve by doing X."

17. Develop, discuss, and keep lists of striving techniques. People have invented many striving techniques, such as "making a special time to do my work," "having a special place to do my work," "asking myself what my mother would say" Anything goes. Some are funny or weird. The list can be kept by the learners in their journals or be put on the wall for all to see. Allotting time for a group discussion from time to time, when appropriate, for group members to share their experiences can be fun and amusing. This technique serves two purposes: first, individuals hear opportunities that might work for them, and have the chance to offer ideas to others; second, and much more important, is that such opportunities build and reinforce the idea and the perception that individuals can and should manage their feelings and motivation to enable them to strive to work energetically toward their goals. They learn that they need not be, and should not be, supine victims of their feelings and moods.

18. Discuss emotional management. Holding individuals responsible for their emotional management can mean taking the time to teach the emotional management process. The time it takes will pay off in many ways, and not just in an increase in internal control. Anger management is an obvious example. In brief, we are not responsible for our feelings, but we are responsible what we DO because of them. For this reason, we are wise to try to control them, moderate them, direct them, ignore them, and/ or, hopefully, to use them. Mad as hell? Figure out what you can do to address the source of your anger, then use your anger as motivation to work like hell. In a bad mood? Stifle it. Be careful what you say. Depressed? Shake yourself out of it. Exercise helps; keep moving. Again, there are two reasons to discuss emotional management. The first is to help learners get specific ideas to use in their lives. The second is to develop and reinforce the idea that they should and can maintain internal control of their feelings, that they should not be and need not be victims of how they feel or of their moods.

19. Offer the opportunity for self-management. When you are teaching internal control you are offering and promoting dignity to those you supervise and train. You offer them the opportunity for self-management and the opportunity to participate as a significant individual in the business in which they are engaged. Take this approach with your learners by stating it this way: "Hey, you want respect? You want to be treated as a person with dignity? Then become responsible. Participate in life and manage yourself." Of course this assumes that you are really providing your learners with a true opportunity to participate and to become self-managed.

20. Use and develop your individual evaluation system to teach and develop internal control. See the evaluation process as a natural time and opportunity to work on learners' internal control skills. Many existing evaluation systems already require internal control behaviors, as per my son's job mentioned earlier. Your evaluation procedures may not be as elaborate as those in a federal agency, but you are free to develop them, to bend this opportunity to your key objective of promoting internal control.

21. Communicate a larger picture of the structure, procedures, and objectives of your organizational activities to your trainees (learners) rather than only the specific activities in which they are engaged. In other words, if your learners are going to become self-managers and exercise internal control they need to have a larger conception of what the company is trying to accomplish. Provide them with information about the larger picture on a regular basis: How is the organization doing? What are its current goals? Is it profitable? How are sales going? Discussion around these kinds of questions builds a sense of participation, of belonging, and of team partnership.

22. Plan group projects together. Talk about the objective tasks, and schedule them out. At the same time, introduce the concepts of internal control as you go. "Okay, now we need to make our goal medium risk. This is a basic rule of organizational planning, and it means that we want to set a goal that we'll have about a 60% chance of achieving. Given our calendar and our other demands, how many widgets do you think we can produce in the coming month?" This is another excellent training opportunity for teaching internal control thinking and behavior.

Conclusion

Now You Can Do It!

CONGRATULATIONS! You are now able to teach internal locus of control.

As a result of reading this book you are now able to teach internal locus of control to others. You can empower those you teach to become Internals, to take control of their lives, to set their own goals, and to work effectively to achieve these same goals.

Let's briefly review what you know.

You know and understand the definition of locus of control and of internality.

You are clear about the many benefits of being an Internal.

You know and understand the Personal Achievement Strategy and you understand the sub-steps of the strategy. For example, you know that when you set goals they should be doable, specific in time, quality, and quantity, and they should be medium risk.

You have read and understood the significance of the research study that validates the effectiveness of the Personal Achievement Strategy as a way to teach internal control.

You are acquainted with suggestions for ways to teach internality that you might use.

And, finally, you are aware of some different situations and venues where teaching internal control could be valuable and could contribute to the greater good.

Amazing! Think of it. You now have the power, the information, and the skill to teach your children, your students, and your employees internality. As a result, and as you know from the research reported in Chapter 2, your learners will most probably experience a higher level of well-being, engage in healthier behavior, be healthier, live longer, and be happier. They will display more motivation to complete tasks, perform well, innovate, and exhibit superior cognitive functioning. They will be more successful in learning and academic achievement and in work and economic endeavors. They will be more active and effective in terms of social and sociological behavior, and they will take responsibility and resist outside influence necessary for moral behavior. And *YOU* will be significantly responsible for this enhancement in the quality of their lives.

Teaching internal control is simple to do. You know how to do it. You know the value of doing it.

So, do it now! *Teach internal locus of control.*

Please stay in touch. As of this writing, I am in the process of establishing the teachinternalcontrol.com website and a Facebook page called "Internal Locus of Control." Both sites will enable us to share resources and explore the activities of those engaged in teaching the Personal Achievement Strategy. I hope to hear from you there.

References

Chapter One

1. Lefcourt, H. M. (1982). *Locus of control: Current trends in theory and research.* (2nd ed.). Hillsdale, NJ: Lawrence Erlbaum Associates.
2. Thomson Reuters, *Social Sciences Citation Index*, 2010.
3. Rotter, J. B. (1966). Generalized expectancies for internal versus external control of reinforcement. *Psychological Monographs*, 80.
4. Bialer, I. (1961). Conceptualization of success and failure in mentally retarded and normative children. *Journal of Personality, 29*, 303–320.
5. Phares, E. J. (1957). Expectancy changes in skill and chance situations. *Journal of Abnormal and Social Psychology, 54*, 339–342.
6. Wallston, B. S., Wallston, K. A., Kaplan, G. D. & Maides, S. A. (1976). Development and validation of the Health Locus of Control (HLC) Scale. *Journal of Consulting and Clinical Psychology, 44*, 580–585.
7. Wallston, K. A. Wallston, B. S. & DeVellis, R. (1978) Development of the Multidimensional Health Locus of Colntrol (MHLC) Scale. *Health Education Monographs, 6*, 160–170.
8. Wallston, K. A. Stein, M. J. & Smith, C. A. (1994). Form C of the MHLC scale: A condition specific measure of locus of control. *Journal of Personality Assessment, 63*, 534–553.
9. Bialer, I. (1961). Conceptualization of success and failure in mentally retarded and normative children. *Journal of Personality, 29*, 303–320.
10. Crandall, V. C., Katkovsky, W. & Crandall, F. J. (1965). Children's belief in their own control of reinforcements in intellectual-academic achievement situations. *Child Development, 36*, 91–109. SHOULDN'T #11 BE LEFCOURT?
11. James, W. H. (1957). Unpublished doctoral dissertation.
12. Nowicki, S. & Strickland, B. R. (1973). A locus of control scale for children. *Journal of Consulting and Clinical Psychology, 40*, 148–155.
13. Reid, D. W. & Ware, E. E. (1974). Multidimensionality of internal versus external control: Addition of a third dimension and non-distinction of self versus others. *Canadian Journal of Behavioral Science, 6*, 131–142.
14. Rotter, J. B. (1966). Generalized expectancies for internal versus external control of reinforcement. *Psychological Monographs, 80*.
15. Mischel, W., Zeiss, R. & Zeiss, A. (1974). Internal–external control and persistence: Validation and implications of the Stanford Preschool Internal-External Scale. *Journal of Personality and Social Psychology, 29*, 265–278.

16. Kirscht, J. P. (1972). Perceptions of control and health belief. *Canadian Journal of Behavioral Science, 4,* 225–237.

17. Levenson, H. (1973). Multidimensional locus of control in psychiatric patients. *Journal of Consulting and Clinical Psychology, 41,* 397–404.

18. Campis, L. K., Lyman, R. D. & Prentice-Dunn (1986). The parental locus of control scale: Development and validation. *Journal of Clinical Child and Adolescent Psychology, 15,* 260–267.

19. Martin, N. J., Holroyd, K. A. & Penzien, D. B. (2005). The headache-specific locus of control scale: Adaptation to recurrent headaches. *Headache: The Journal of Head and Face Pain, 30,* 729–734.

20. Ozkan, T., Lajunen, T. (2005). Multidimensional traffic locus of control scale (T-LOC): Factor structure and relationship to risky driving. *Personality and Individual Differences, 38,* 533–545.

21. Donovan, D. M. & O'Leary, M. R. (1978). The drinking-related locus of control scale. *Journal of Studies on Alcohol, 39,* 759–784.

22. Haine, R. A., Ayers, T. S., Sandler, I. N., Wolchik, S. A. & Weyer, J. L. (2003). Locus of control and self-esteem as stress-moderators or stress-mediators in parentally bereaved children. *Death Studies, 27,* 619–640.

23. Abramson, L. Y., Seligman, M. E. P. & Teasdale, J. D. (1978). Learned helplessness in humans: Critique and reformulation. *Journal of Abnormal Psychology, 87,* 49–74.

24. Vander Schee, B. A. (2009). Do students really know their academic strengths? *Teaching Professor, 23,* 2.

25. Uguak, U. A., Elias, H., Uli, J. & Suandi, T. (2007). The influence of causal elements of locus of control on academic achievement satisfaction. *Journal of Instructional Psychology, 34,* 120–128.

26. Njus, D. M. & Brockway, J. H. (1999). Perceptions of competence and locus of control for positive and negative outcomes. *Personality and Individual Differences, 26,* 531–548.

27. Heineck, G. & Anger, S. (2010). The returns to cognitive abilities and personality traits in Germany. *Labour Economics, 17,* 535–546.

28. Nickasch, B & Marnocha, S. K. (2009). Healthcare experiences of the homeless. *Journal of the American Academy of Nurse Practitioners, 21,* 39–46.

29. Reimers-Hild, C. (2007). 'Entrepreneurial' qualities help online learners succeed. *Online Classroom,* 2–5.

30. Baumeister, R. F., Campbell, J. D., Krueger, J. I. & Vohs, K. D. (2005). Exploding the self-esteem myth. *Scientific American, 292,* 84–91.

31. Habibollah, N., Rohani, A., Aizan, H. T., Jamaluddin, S & Kumar, V. (2009). Self esteem, gender and academic achievement of undergraduate students. *American Journal of Scientific Research,* 26–37.

32. Booth, M., & Gerard, J. (2009). Academic achievement and self-image: A comparative study of adolescent students in the US and UK. *Proceedings of the Annual meeting of the 53rd annual conference of the comparative and international education society* Charleston: SC.

33. Baumeister, R. F., Campbell, J. D., Kreuger, J. I. & Vohs, K. D. (2003). Does

high self-esteem cause better performance, interpersonal success, happiness, or healthier lifestyles? *Psychological Science in the Public Interest, 4,* 1–44.

34. Huitt, W. (2009). Self-concept and self-esteem. *Educational Psychology Interactive.* Valdosta, GA: Valdosta State University. Retrieved [12/13/2010] from http://www.edpsycinteractive.org/topics/regsys/self.html.

35. Joshi, S. & Srivastava, R. (2009). Self-esteem and academic achievement of adolescents. *Journal of the Indian Academy of Applied Psychology, 35,* 33–39.

36. Lefcourt, H. M. (1982). *Locus of control: Current trends in theory and research.* (2nd ed.). Hillsdale, NJ: Lawrence Erlbaum Associates.

37. Lefcourt, H. M. (1982). *Locus of control: Current trends in theory and research.* (2nd ed.). Hillsdale, NJ: Lawrence Erlbaum Associates.

38. Borman, G. D. & Rachuba, L. T. (2001). *Academic success among poor and minority students: An analysis of competing models of school effects.* Center for Research on the Education of Students Placed at Risk, Baltimore, MD.

39. Nickasch, B & Marnocha, S. K. (2009). Healthcare experiences of the homeless. *Journal of the American Academy of Nurse Practitioners, 21,* 39–46.

40. Battle, E. & Rotter, J. B. (1963). Children's feelings of personal control as related to social class and ethnic group. *Journal of Personality, 31,* 482–490.

41. Borman, G. D. & Rachuba, L. T. (2001). *Academic success among poor and minority students: An analysis of competing models of school effects.* Center for Research on the Education of Students Placed at Risk, Baltimore, MD.

42. Howerton, D, Enger, J, & Wynn, C. (1992). Locus of control and achievement of at-risk adolescent black males. *Proceedings of the Annual meeting of the mid-south educational research association* Knoxville: TN.

43. Otterman, Y. (2002). The great culture debate: Clearly not a black and white issue. *Tutorial produced for Psy 324, Advanced Social Psychology, Miami University, Miama, FL.* Retrieved [12/13/2010] from http://www.units.muohio.edu/psybersite/control/culture.shtml.

44. Graham, S. (1994). Ethnicity, gender, and family income. *Review of Educational Research.*

45. Malcarne, V. L., Drahota, A. & Hamilton, N. A. (2005). Children's health-related locus of control beliefs: Ethnicity, gender, and family income. *Children's Health Care, 34,* 47–59.

46. Cohen, E., Biran, G., Aran, A. & Gross-Tsur, V. (2008). Locus of control, perceived parenting style, and anxiety in children with cerebral palsy. *Journal of Developmental and Physical Disability, 20,* 415–423.

47. McCabe, K. M., Goehring, K., Yeh, M. & Lau, A. S. (2008). Parental locus of control and externalizing behavior problems among Mexican American preschoolers. *Journal of Emotional and Behavioral Disorders, 16,* 118–126.

48. Khayyer, M. & Alborzi, S. Locus of control of children experiencing separation and divorce in their families in Iran. *Psychological Reports, 90,* 239–242.

49. Lifshitz, M. (1973). Internal-external locus-of-control dimension as a function of age and the socialization milieu. *Child Development, 44,* 538–546.

50. Nowicki, S. & Barnes, J. (1973). Effects of a structured camp experience on locus of control orientation. *Journal of Genetic Psychology, 122,* 247–252.

51. Pierce, R. M., Schauble, P. G. & Farkas, A. (1973). Teaching internalization behavior to clients. *Psychotherapy: Theory Research and Practice, 7,* 217–220.

52. deCharms, R. (1973). Intervention is impossible: A model for change from within. *School Intervention.* New York: Behavioral Publications.

53. Hill, R. A. (1978). Internality: An educational imperative. *Journal of Humanistic Psychology, 18,* 43–57.

54. Reimanis, G. (1970). A study of home environment and readiness for achievement at school. Final report.

55. McClelland, D. C. (1961). *The Achieving Society.* Princeton, NJ: VanNostrand.

56. Hong, S., Sukkyung, Y., Eun-Joo, K. & Joohan, K. (2008). Multivariate autoregressive cross-lagged modeling of the reciprocal longitudinal relationship between perceived control and academic achievement. *Psychological Reports, 102,* 873–883.

57. Coleman, J. S., Campbell, E. G., Hobsom, C. J., McPartland, J., Alexander, M., Weinfield, F. D. & York, R. L. (1966). *Equality of education opportunity.* Washington, D.C.: Department of Health, Education and Welfare.

Chapter 2

1. Pannells, T. C. & Claxton, A. F. (2008). Happiness, creative ideation and locus of control. *Creativity Research Journal, 20,* 67–71.

2. Findley, M. J. & Cooper, H. M. (1983). Locus of control and academic achievement: A literature review. *Journal of Personality and Social Psychology, 44,* 419–427.

3. Frantz, R. S. (1980). Internal-external locus of control and labor market performance: Empirical evidence using longitudinal survey data. *Psychology: A Quarterly Journal of Human Behavior, 17,* 23–29.

4. Viera Jr., E. T. & Grantham, S. (2009). Antecedent influences on children's extrinsic motivation to go online. *Journal of Applied Social Psychology, 39,* 707–733.

5. Cotter, R. P. (2003). High risk behavior in adolescence and their relationship to death anxiety and death personification. *Omega: Journal of Death and Dying, 47,* 119–137.

6. Kopp, R. G. & Ruzicka, M. F. (1993). Women's multiple roles and psychological well-being. *Psychological Reports, 72,* 1351–1355.

7. Loree, T., & Stupka, E. (1993). Teaching and learning in a student success course: a discussion concerning the development of the internal locus of control using fuzzy logic, TQM, and the chaos theory of education. *Proceedings of the National Conference on Teaching and Learning,* Arlington: VA.

8. Martin, J. C. (1978). Locus of control and self-esteem in Indian and White students. *Journal of American Indian Education, 18.*

9. Reznikoff, M., Bridges, C., & Hirsch, T. (1972). Internal-external control orientation, self-description, and bridge-playing expertise. *Psychology Reports, 31,* 683–689.

10. Roberts, A. (1971). *The self-esteem disadvantage of third- and seventh-graders.*

Unpublished doctoral dissertation, Emory University.

11. Warehime, R. G. & Foulds, M. F. (1971). Perceived locus of control and personal adjustment. *Journal of Consulting and Clinical Psychology, 37,* 250–252.

12. Fish, B & Karabenick, S. A. (1971). Relationship between self-esteem and locus of control. *Psychological Reports, 29,* 784.

13. Shybut, J. (1970). Internal versus external control, time perspective, and delay of gratification of high and low ego strength groups. *Journal of Clinical Psychology, 26,* 430–431.

14. Abramowitz, S. I. (1969). Locus of control and self-reported depression among college students. *Psychological Reports, 25,* 149–150.

15. Platt, J. J. & Eiseman, R. (1968). Internal-external control of reinforcement, time, perspective, adjustment and anxiety. *Journal of General Psychology,79,* 121–128.

16. Hersch, P. D. & Scheibe, K. E. (1967). Reliability and validity of internal-external control as a personality dimension. *Journal of Consulting Psychology, 31,* 609–613.

17. Battle, E. & Rotter, J. B. (1963). Children's feelings of personal control as related to social class and ethnic group. *Journal of Personality, 31,* 482–490.

18. Aberle, I., Scholz, U., Bach-Kliegel, B., Fischer, C., Gorney, M., Langer, K. & Kliegel, M. Psychological aspects in continuous subcutaneous insulin infusion: A retrospective study. *Journal of Psychology, 143,* 147–160.

19. Al-Turkait, F. A. & Ohaeri, J. U. (2008). Prevalence and correlates of posttraumatic stress disorder among Kuwaiti military men according to level of involvement in the first Gulf War. *Depression & Anxiety, 25,* 932–941.

20. Cohen, E., Sade, M., Benarroch, F., Pollak, Y. & Gross-Tsur, V. (2008). Locus of control, perceived parenting style and symptoms of anxiety and depression in children with Tourette's syndrome. *European Child and Adolescent Psychiatry, 17,* 299–305.

21. Heath, R. L., Saliba, M., Mahmassani, O., Major, S. C. & Khoury, B. A. (2008). Locus of control moderates the relationship between headache pain and depression. *Journal of Headache and Pain, 9,* 301–308.

22. Pipinelli, A. (2006). Psychological variable and depression among nursing home and adult care facility residence. *Dissertation Abstracts International: Section B: The Sciences and Engineering, 66,* 4496.

23. Tsuboi, S., Fukukawa, Y., Niino, N., Ando, F. & Shimokata, H. (2004). Age and gender differences in factors related to depressive symptoms among community-dwelling, middle-aged and elderly people. *Japanese Journal of Psychology, 75,* 101–108.

24. Hammond, W. A. & Romney, D. M. (1995). Cognitive factors contributing to adolescent depression. *Journal of Youth and Adolescence, 24,* 667–683.

25. Weisz, J. R. (1990). Development of control-related beliefs, goals, and styles in childhood and adolescence. Carmi Schooler (Ed.) *Self-directedness, Cause and effects throughout the life course.* Hillsdale, N.J., U.S.A. Lawrence Erlbaum Associates Inc.

26. Benassi, V. A., Sweeney, P. D. & Dufour, C. L. (1988). Is there a relation between locus of control orientation and depression? *Journal of Abnormal Psychology, 97,* 357–367.

27. Tomlinson, L. M. (1987). Locus of control and its affect on achievement.

28. Banks, L. M. III & Goggin, W. C. (1983). The relationship of locus of control and attribution to depression. *Proceedings from the Annual Meeting of the South-Eastern Psychological Association* Atlanta: GA.

29. Hiroto, D. S. (1974). Locus of control and learned helplessness. *Journal of Experimental Psychology, 102,* 187–193.

30. Abramowitz, S. I. (1969). Locus of control and self-reported depression among college students. *Psychological Reports, 25,* 149–150.

31. Lauer, S., de Man, A. F., Marquez, S. & Ades, J. (2008). External locus of control, problem-focused coping and attempted suicide. *North American Journal of Psychology, 10,* 625–632.

32. Varma, G., Acar, K., Ozdel, O., Kurtulus, A., Yucel, E. & Oguzhanoglu, N. K. (2007). Relationship between locus of control and suicide attempt. *Tükiye'de Psikiyatri, 9,* 79–83.

33. Burger, J. M. (2006). Desire for control, locus of control, and proneness to depression. *Journal of Personality, 52,* 71–89.

34. Spann, M., Molock, S. D., Barksdale, C., Matlin, S. & Puri, R. (2006). Suicide and African American teenagers: Risk factors and coping mechanisms. *Suicide and Life-Threatening Behavior, 36,* 553–568.

35. Evans, W. P., Owens, P. & Marsh, S. C. (2005). Environmental factors, locus of control and adolescent suicide risk. *Child & Adolescent Social Work Journal, 22,* 301–319.

36. Martin, G., Richardson, A. S., Bergen, H. A., Roeger, L. & Allison S. (2005). Perceived academic performance, self-esteem and locus of control as indicators of need for assessment of adolescent suicide risk: Implications for teachers. *Journal of Adolescence, 28,* 75–87.

37. Beautrais, A. L. T., Joyce, P. R. & Mulder, R. T. (1999). Personality traits and cognitive styles as risk factors for serious suicide attempts among young people. *Suicide and Life-Threatening Behavior, 29,* 37–47.

38. Williams, C. B. & Nickels, J. B. (1969). Internal-external control dimensions as related to accident and suicide proneness. *Journal of Consulting and Clinical Psychology, 33,* 485–494.

39. Li, H. C. W. & Chung, O. K. J. (2009). The relationship between children's locus of control and their anticipatory anxiety. *Public Health Nursing, 26,* 153–60.

40. Dilmac, B., Hamarta, E. & Arslan, C. (2009). Analysing the trait anxiety and locus of control of undergraduates in terms of attachment styles. *Educational Sciences: Theory & Practice, 9,* 143–159.

41. Lloyd, T. & Hastings, R. P. (2009). Parental locus of control and psychological well-being in mothers of children with intellectual disability. *Journal of Intellectual and Developmental Disability, 34,* 104–115.

42. Scrimin, S., Haynes, M., Alto, G., Bornstein, M. H. & Axia, G. (2009). Anxiety and stress in mothers and fathers in the 24 h after their child's surgery. *Child: Care, Health and Development, 35,* 227–233.

43. Al-Turkait, F. A. & Ohaeri, J. U. (2008). Prevalence and correlates of posttraumatic stress disorder among Kuwaiti military men according to level of

involvement in the first Gulf War. *Depression & Anxiety, 25,* 932–941.

44. Cohen, E., Sade, M., Benarroch, F., Pollak, Y. & Gross-Tsur, V. (2008). Locus of control, perceived parenting style and symptoms of anxiety and depression in children with Tourette's syndrome. *European Child and Adolescent Psychiatry, 17,* 299–305.

45. Naditch, M. P. (1973). Locus of control, relative discontent, and hypertension. *Proceedings of the 81st Annual Convention of the American Psychological Association, 8,* 295–296.

46. Powell, A. & Vega, M. (1972). Correlated of adult locus of control. *Psychological Reports, 30,* 455–460.

47. Platt, J. J. & Eiseman, R. (1968). Internal-external control of reinforcement, time, perspective, adjustment and anxiety. *Journal of General Psychology, 79,* 121–128.

48. Feather, N. T. (1967). Some personality correlates of external control. *Australian Journal of Psychology, 19,* 253–260.

49. Tolor, A. & Reznikoff, M. (1967). Relations between insight, repression-sensitization, internal-external locus of control and death anxiety. *Journal of Abnormal Psychology, 72,* 426–430.

50. Watson, D. (1967). Relationship between locus of control and anxiety. *Journal of Personality and Social Psychology, 6,* 91–92.

51. Watson, D. & Baumal, E. (1967). Effects of locus of control and expectation of future control upon present performance. *Journal of Personality and Social Psychology, 6,* 212–215.

52. Butterfield, E. C. (1964). Locus of control, test anxiety, reactions to frustration, and achievement attitudes. *Journal of Personality, 32,* 355–370.

53. Nowicki, S. & Roundtree, J. (1971). Correlates of locus of control in secondary school age students. *Developmental Psychology, 4,* 479.

54. Shipe, D. (1971). Impulsivity and locus of control as predictors of achievement and adjustment in mildly retarded and borderline youth. *American Journal of Mental Deficiency, 76,* 12–22.

55. Platt, J. J. & Eiseman, R. (1968). Internal-external control of reinforcement, time, perspective, adjustment and anxiety. *Journal of General Psychology, 79,* 121–128.

56. Hersch, P. D. & Scheibe, K. E. (1967). Reliability and validity of internal-external control as a personality dimension. *Journal of Consulting Psychology, 31,* 609–613.

57. Phares, E. J. (1965). Internal-external control as a determinant of amount of social influence exerted. *Journal of Personality and Social Psychology, 2,* 642–647.

58. Lefcourt, H. M., Sordoni, C. & Sordoni, C. (1974). Locus of control and the expression of humor. *Journal of Personality, 42,* 130–143.

59. Reznikoff, M., Bridges, C., & Hirsch, T. (1972). Internal-external control orientation, self-description, and bridge-playing expertise. *Psychology Reports, 31,* 683–689.

60. Davis, W. L. & Davis, D. E. (1972). Internal-external control and attribution responsibility for success and failure. *Journal of Personality, 40,* 123–136.

61. Phares, E. J. & Wilson, K. G. (1972). Responsibility attributed: Role of outcome severity, situational ambiguity, and internal-external locus of control. *Journal of Personality, 40,* 392–406.

62. Phares, E. J. (1971). Internal-external control and the reduction of reinforcement value after failure. *Journal of Consulting and Clinical Psychology, 37,* 386–390.

63. Phares, E. J., Ritchie, D. E. & Davis, W. L. (1968). Internal-external locus of control and reaction to threat. *Journal of Personality and Social Psychology, 10,* 402–405.

64. Efran, J. S. (1963). Some personality determinants of memory success and failure. (Unpublished doctoral dissertation) Ohio State University, OH.

65. Brissett, M. & Nowicki, S. (1973). Internal versus external control of reinforcement and reaction to frustration. *Journal of Personality and Social Psychology, 25,* 35–44.

66. Phares, E. J., Ritchie, D. E. & Davis, W. L. (1968). Internal-external locus of control and reaction to threat. *Journal of Personality and Social Psychology, 10,* 402–405.

67. Phares, E. J., Ritchie, D. E. & Davis, W. L. (1968). Internal-external locus of control and reaction to threat. *Journal of Personality and Social Psychology, 10,* 402–405.

68. Mellon, R. C., Papanikolau, V. & Prodromitis, G. (2009). Locus of control and psychopathology in relation to levels of trauma and loss: Self-report of Peloponnesian wildfire survivors. *Journal of Traumatic Stress, 22,* 189,196.

69. Ross, L. T. & Miller, J. R. (2009). Parental divorce and college students: The impact of family unpredictability and perceptions of divorce. *Journal of Divorce and Remarriage, 50,* 248–259.

70. Al-Turkait, F. A. & Ohaeri, J. U. (2008). Prevalence and correlates of posttraumatic stress disorder among Kuwaiti military men according to level of involvement in the first Gulf War. *Depression & Anxiety, 25,* 932–941.

71. Chen, J. & Wang, L. (2007). Locus of control and the three components of commitment to change. *Personality and Individual Differences, 42,* 503–512.

72. Cannon, J. T. (2003). Experiences of the 1989 Loma Prieta earthquake: A narrative analysis. *Dissertation Abstracts International: Section B: The Sciences and Engineering, 64,* 1938.

73. Kurland, L. (2003). A qualitative analysis of sibling loss by sudden death during adolescence. *Dissertation Abstracts International: Section B: The Sciences and Engineering, 64,* 2392.

74. Mellon, R. C., Papanikolau, V. & Prodromitis, G. (2009). Locus of control and psychopathology in relation to levels of trauma and loss: Self-report of Peloponnesian wildfire survivors. *Journal of Traumatic Stress, 22,* 189,196.

75. Gale, C. R., Battty, D. & Deary, I. J. (2008). Locus of control at age 10 years and health outcomes and behaviors at age 30 years: The 1970 British cohort study. *Psychosomatic Medicine, 70,* 379–403.

76. Levenson, H. (1973). Multidimensional locus of control in psychiatric patients. *Journal of Consulting and Clinical Psychology, 41,* 397–404.

77. Altin, M. & Karanci, A. N. (2008). How does locus of control and inflated sense of responsibility relate to obsessive-compulsive symptoms in Turkish adolescents? *Journal of Anxiety Disorders, 22,* 1303–1315.

78. Mei-Yu, Y. (2008). Measuring readiness to change and locus of control belief among male alcohol-dependent patients is Taiwan: Comparison of the different degrees of alcohol dependence. *Psychiatry and Clinical Neuroscience, 62,* 533–539.

79. Yeh, M. (2008). Measuring readiness to change and locus of control belief among male alcohol-dependent patients in Taiwan: Comparison of the different degrees of alcohol dependence. *Psychiatry and Clinical Neuroscience, 62,* 533–539.

80. Al-Turkait, F. A. & Ohaeri, J. U. (2008). Prevalence and correlates of posttraumatic stress disorder among Kuwaiti military men according to level of involvement in the first Gulf War. *Depression & Anxiety, 25,* 932–941.

81. Horesh, N., Zalsman, G. & Apter, A. (2000). Internalized anger, self control, and mastery experience in inpatient anorexic adolescents. *Journal of Psychosomatic Research, 49,* 247–253.

82. Wojciak, R. W., Mojs, E. & Cierpialkowska, L. (2009). The health locus of control in anorexic women. *European Psychiatry, 24,* 764.

83. Watson, D. C. (1998). The relationship of self-esteem, locus of control and dimensional models to personality disorders. *Journal of Social Behavior and Personality, 13,* 399–420.

84. Modestin, J., Caveng, I., Wehril, M. V. & Malti, T. (2008). Correlates of coping styles in psychotic illness – An extension study. *Psychiatry Research, 168,* 50–56.

85. Furnham, A., Jensen, T & Crump, J. (2008). Personality, intelligence and assessment centre expert ratings. *International Journal of Selection and Assessment, 16,* 356–365.

86. Langan-Fox, J., Sankey, M. J. & Canty, J. M. (2009). Incongruence between implicit and self-attributed achievement motives and psychological well-being: The moderating role of self-directedness, self disclosure and locus of control.

87. Lloyd, T. & Hastings, R. P. (2009). Parental locus of control and psychological well-being in mothers of children with intellectual disability. *Journal of Intellectual and Developmental Disability, 34,* 104–115.

88. Judge, T. A. (2009). Core self-evaluations and work success. *Current Directions in Psychological Science,18,* 58–62.

89. Scrimin, S., Haynes, M., Alto, G., Bornstein, M. H. & Axia, G. (2009). Anxiety and stress in mothers and fathers in the 24 h after their child's surgery. *Child: Care, Health and Development, 35,* 227–233.

90. Glenn, S., Cunningham, C., Poole, H., Reeves, D. & Weindling, M. (2009). Maternal parenting stress and its correlates in families with a young child with cerebral palsy. *Child: Care, Health and Development, 35,* 71–78.

91. Cunningham, J. Just relax. *Professional Engineering, 19,* 33.

92. Huang, H. (2006). Understanding culinary art workers: Locus of control, job satisfaction, work stress and turnover intention. *Journal of Foodservice Business Research, 9,* 151–168.

93. Owen, S. S. (2006). Occupational stress among correctional supervisors. *Prison Journal, 86,* 164–181.

94. Schmitz, N., Neumann, W. & Oppermann, R. (2000). Stress, burnout and locus of control in German nurses. *International Journal of Nursing Studies, 37,* 93–99.

95. Gizir, C. A. & Aydin, G. (2009). Protective factors contributing to the academic resilience of students living in poverty in Turkey. *Professional School Counseling, 13,* 38–49.

96. Efta-Breitbach, J. & Freeman, K. A. (2004).Recidivism and resilience in juvenile sex offenders: An analysis of the literature. *Journal of Child Sexual Abuse, 13,* 257–279.

97. Kurland, L. (2003). A qualitative analysis of sibling loss by sudden death during adolescence. *Dissertation Abstracts International: Section B: The Sciences and Engineering, 64,* 2392.

98. Lynch, S., Hurford, D. P. & Cole, A. (2002). Parental enabling attitudes and internal locus of control of at-risk honors students. *Adolescence, 37,* 527–549.

99. Borman, G. D. & Rachuba, L. T. (2001). *Academic success among poor and minority students: An analysis of competing models of school effects.* Center for Research on the Education of Students Placed at Risk, Baltimore, MD.

100. Dalgard, O. S., Bork, S. & Tambs, K. (1995). Social support, negative life events and mental health. *The British Journal of Psychiatry, 166,* 29–34.

101. Lester, D., Aldridge, M., Aspenberg, C., Boyle, K., Radsniak, P. & Waldron, C. (2001). What is the afterlife like? Undergraduate beliefs about the afterlife. *Omega: Journal of Death and Dying, 44,* 113–126.

102. Barbuto Jr., J. E. & Story, J. S. (2008). Relations between locus of control and sources of work motivation amongst government workers. *Psychological Reports, 102,* 335–338.

103. Ghorpade, J., Lackritz, J. & Singh, G. (2006). Correlates of the Protestant ethic of hard work: Results from a diverse ethno-religious sample. *Journal of Applied Social Psychology, 36,* 249–2473.

104. Laptosky, G. (2002). Locus of control and type of reinforcement as factors in human response to noncontingency. *Dissertation Abstracts International: Section B: The Sciences and Engineering, 62,* 4205.

105. Reeve, J., Nix, G. & Hamm, D. (2003). Testing models of the experience if self-determination in intrinsic motivation and conundrum of choice. *Journal of Educational Psychology 95,* 375–392.

106. Hadsel, L. (2010). Achievement goals, locus of control, and academic success in economics. *American Economic Review, 100,* 272–276.

107. Landrum, R. E. (2010). Intent to apply to graduate school: Perceptions of senior year psychology majors. *North American Journal of Psychology, 12,* 243–254.

108. Sidelinger, R. J. (2010). College student involvement: An examination of student characteristics and perceived instructor communication behaviors in the classroom. *Communication Studies, 61,* 87–103.

109. Deniz, M. E., Tras, Z & Aydogan, D. (2009). An investigation of academic procrastination, locus of control, and emotional intelligence. *Educational Sciences: Theory and Practice, 9,* 623–632.

110. Harsch, D. M. (2009). The role of self-efficacy, locus of control, and self handicapping in dissertation completion. *Dissertation Abstracts International Section A: Humanities and Social Sciences, 69,* 4261.

111. Nordstrom, C. R. & Segrist, D. J. (2009). Predicting the likelihood of going to

graduate school: The importance of locus of control. *College Student Journal, 43,* 200–206.

112. Wang, X. (2009). Baccalaureate attainment and college persistence of community college transfer students at four-year institutions. *Research in Higher Education, 50,* 570–588.

113. Hall, C., Smith, K. & Chia, R. (2008). Cognitive and personality factors in relation to timely completion of a college degree. *College Student Journal, 42,* 1087–1098.

114. Hand, C. & Payne, E. M. (2008). First-generation college students: A study of Appalachian student success. *Journal of Developmental Education, 32,* 4–15.

115. Kingston, E. (2008). Emotional competence and drop-out rates in higher education. *Education & Training, 50,* 128–139.

116. Sciarra, D. T. & Whitson, M. L. (2007). Predictive factors in postsecondary educational attainment among Latinos. *Professional School Counseling, 10,* 1096–2409.

117. Benham, J. M. (1995). Fostering self motivated behavior, personal responsibility, and internal locus of control in the school setting.

118. Skinner, E. A., Wellborn, J. G. & Connell, J. P. (1990). What it takes to do well in school and whether I've got it: A process model of perceived control and children's engagement and achievement in school. *Journal of Educational Psychology, 82,* 22–32.

119. Harsch, D. M. (2009). The role of self-efficacy, locus of control, and self handicapping in dissertation completion. *Dissertation Abstracts International Section A: Humanities and Social Sciences, 69,* 4261.

120. Wang, X. (2009). Baccalaureate attainment and college persistence of community college transfer students at four-year institutions. *Research in Higher Education, 50,* 570–588.

121. Blanchard, A. L. & Henle, C. A. (2008). Correlates of different forms of cyberloafing: The role of norms and external locus of control. *Computers in Human Behavior, 24,* 1067–1084.

122. Keller, J. & Blomann, F. (2008). Locus of control and the flow experience: An experimental analysis. *European Journal of Personality, 22,* 589–607.

123. Gurol, Y. & Atsan, N. (2006). Entrepreneurial characteristics amongst university students: Some insights for entrepreneurial education and training in Turkey. *Education & Training, 48,* 25–38.

124. Ng, T. W. H., Sorensen, K. L. & Eby, L. T. (2006). Locus of control at work: A meta-analysis. *Journal of Organizational Behavior, 27,* 1057–1087.

125. Erwee, R. (1986). Achievement motivation and locus of control of Black University students. *Journal of Industrial Psychology, 12.*

126. Baron, R. M. & Ganz, R. L. (1972). Effects of locus of control and the type of feedback on the task performance of lower-class black children. *Journal of Personality and Social Psychology, 21,* 124–130.

127. Blanchard, A. L. & Henle, C. A. (2008). Correlates of different forms of cyberloafing: The role of norms and external locus of control. *Computers in Human Behavior, 24,* 1067–1084.

128. Gurol, Y. & Atsan, N. (2006). Entrepreneurial characteristics amongst university students: Some insights for entrepreneurial education and training in Turkey. *Education & Training, 48,* 25–38.

129. Ng, T. W. H., Sorensen, K. L. & Eby, L. T. (2006). Locus of control at work: A meta-analysis. *Journal of Organizational Behavior, 27,* 1057–1087.

130. Spector, P. E. (1982). Behavior in organizations as a function of employee's locus of control. *Psychological Bulletin, 91,* 482–497.

131. Fogel, J. & Israel, S. (2009). Consumer attitudes regarding internet health information and communication: Gender, locus of control, and stress implications. *Internet Journal of Clinical and Health Psychology, 9,* 275–286.

132. Hashimoto, H. & Fukuhara, S. (2004). The influence of locus of control on preferences for information and decision making. *Patient Education and Counseling, 55,* 236–240.

133. Williams, J. G. (1970). Internal-external control as a situational variable in determining information-seeking by Negro students. (Unpublished doctoral dissertation). George Peabody Teachers College, Nashville.

134. Davis, W. L. & Phares, E. J. (1967). Internal-external control as a determinant of information-seeking in a social influence situation. *Journal of Personality, 35,* 547–561.

135. DuCette, J. & Wolk, S. (1973). Cognitive and motivational correlates of generalized expectancies for control. *Journal of Personality and Social Psychology, 26,* 420–426.

136. Ude, L. K. & Vogler, R. E. (1969). Internal versus external control of reinforcement and awareness in a conditioning task. *Journal of Psychology, 73,* 63–67.

137. Lefcourt, H. M. (1967). Effects of cue explication upon persons maintaining external control expectancies. *Journal of Personality and Social Psychology, 5,* 372–378.

138. Seeman, M. (1967). On the personal consequences of alienation in work. *American Sociological Review, 32,* 273–285(a).

139. Seeman, M. (1963). Alienation and social learning in a reformatory. *American Journal of Sociology, 69,* 270–284.

140. Seeman, M. & Evans, J. W. (1962). Alienation and learning in a hospital setting. *American Sociological Review, 27,* 772–782.

141. Kesici, S., Sahin, I. & Akturk, A. O. (2009). Analysis of cognitive learning strategies and computer attitudes, according to college students' gender and locus of control. *Computers in Human Behavior, 25,* 529–534.

142. Onwuegbuzie, A. J. & Daley, C. E. (1998). Study skills of graduates as a function of academic locus of control, self-perception, and social interdependence. *Psychological Reports, 83,* 595–598.

143. Bartel, H., Ducette, J. & Wolk, S. (1972) Category clustering in free recall and locus of control. *Journal of General Psychology, 87,* 251–257.

144. Doron, J., Stephan, Y., Boiche, J. & Le Scanff, C. (2009). Coping with examinations. Exploring relationships between students' coping strategies, implicit theories of ability, and perceived control. *British Journal of Educational*

Psychology, 79, 515–528.

145. Akinsola, M. K. (2008). Relationship of some psychological variables in predicting problem solving ability of in-service mathematics teachers. *The Montana Mathematics Enthusiast, 5*, 79–100.

146. Morry, M. M. & Harasymchuk, C. (2005). Perceptions of locus of control and satisfaction in friendship: The impact of problem-solving strategies. *Journal of Social and Personal Relationships, 22*,183–206.

147. Phares, E. J., Ritchie, D. E. & Davis, W. L. (1968). Internal-external locus of control and reaction to threat. *Journal of Personality and Social Psychology, 10*, 402–405.

148. Tolor, A. & Reznikoff, M. (1967). Relations between insight, repression-sensitization, internal-external locus of control and death anxiety. *Journal of Abnormal Psychology, 72*, 426–430.

149. Shipe, D. (1971). Impulsivity and locus of control as predictors of achievement and adjustment in mildly retarded and borderline youth. *American Journal of Mental Deficiency, 76*, 12–22.

150. Baiocco, R., Laghi, F. & D'Alessio, M. (2009). Decision-making style among adolescents: Relationship with sensation seeking and locus of control. *Journal of Adolescence, 32*, 963–976.

151. Yurtsever, G. Measuring moral imagination. *Social Behavior and Personality: An International Journal, 34*, 205–219.

152. Martin, J. E. (1991). The relationship among internal-external locus of control and rational-irrational beliefs. *Proceedings of the Annual meeting of the mid-south educational research association* Knoxville: TN.

153. Martin, J. E. (1992). The effects of internal-external locus of control and selected demographic variables on rational-irrational beliefs. *Proceedings of the Annual Meeting of the Mid-South Educational Research Association*, Knoxville: TN.

154. Clouser, R. A. & Hjelle, L. A. (1970). Relationship between locus of control and dogmatism. *Psychological Reports, 26*, 1006.

155. Brecher, M. & Denmark, F. L. (1969). Internal-external locus of control and verbal fluency. *Psychological Reports, 25*, 707–710.

156. Libert, Y., Merckart, I., Reynaert, C., Delvaux, N., Marchal, S., Etienne, A., Boniver, J., Klatersky, J., Scalliet, P., Slachmuylder J, & Razavi, D. (2007). Physicians are different when they learn communication skills: Influence of the locus of control.

157. Rubin, A. M. (1993). The effect of locus of control on communication motivation, anxiety, and satisfaction. *Communication Quarterly, 41*, 161–171.

158. Amrhein, P. C., Bond, J. K. & Hamilton, D. A. (1999). Locus of control and age difference in free recall from episodic memory. *The Journal of General Psychology, 126*, 149–164.

159. Riggs, K. M., Lachman, M. E. & Wingfield, A. (1997). Taking charge of remembering: Locus of control and older adults' memory for speech. *Experimental Aging Research, 23*, 237–256.

160. West, R. L., Dak-Freudeman, A. & Bagwell, D. K. (2009). Goals-feedback conditions and episodic memory: Mechanisms for memory gains in older and

younger adults. *Memory, 17,* 233–244.

161. Matud, M. P., Bethancourt, J. M., Ibanez, I., Lopez, M., Rodriguez, C. & Grande, J. (2006). Relevance of motivation and locus of control variables for creative thinking in men and women from the general population. *Analisis y Modificacion de Conducta, 32,* 643–660.

162. Vander Schee, B. A. (2009). Do students really know their academic strengths? *Teaching Professor, 23,* 2.

163. Uguak, U. A., Elias, H., Uli, J. & Suandi, T. (2007). The influence of causal elements of locus of control on academic achievement satisfaction. *Journal of Instructional Psychology, 34,* 120–128.

164. Njus, D. M. & Brockway, J. H. (1999). Perceptions of competence and locus of control for positive and negative outcomes. *Personality and Individual Differences, 26,* 531–548.

165. McLean, R. (1997). Selected attitudinal factors relating to students' success in high school. *Alberta Journal of Educational Research, 43,* 165–168.

166. Karnes, F. A. & McGinnis J. C. (1996). Self-actualization and locus of control with academically talented adolescents. *Journal of Secondary Gifted Education, 7,* 369–372.

167. Sterbin, A. & Rakow, E. (1996). Self-esteem, locus of control, and student achievement. *Proceedings of the Annual Meeting of the Mid-South Educational Research Association,* Tuscaloosa: AL.

168. Knight, B. A. (1995). The influence of locus of control on gifted and talented students. *Gifted Education International, 11,* 31–33.

169. Shell, D. F., Colvin, C. & Brunning, R. H. (1995). Self-efficacy, attribution, and outcome expectancy mechanisms in reading and writing achievement: Grade level and achievement-level differences. *Journal of Educational Psychology, 87,* 386–398.

170. Zimmerman, B. J. & Bandura, A. (1994). Impact of self-regulatory influences on writing course attainment. *American Educational Research Journal, 87,* 845–862.

171. Randhawa, B. S., Beamer, J. E. & Lungberg, I. (1993). Role of mathematics self-efficacy in the structural model of mathematics Achievement. *Journal of Educational Psychology, 85,* 41–48.

172. Foley, R. M. & Epstein, M. (1992). Correlates of the academic achievement of adolescents with behavioral disorders. *Behavioral Disorders, 18,* 9–17.

173. Howerton, D, Enger, J, & Wynn, C. (1992). Locus of control and achievement of at-risk adolescent black males. *Proceedings of the Annual meeting of the mid-south educational research association* Knoxville: TN.

174. Creek, R. J. (1991). Internality and achievement in the intermediate grades. Cunningham, J. Just relax. *Professional Engineering, 19,* 33.

175. Butler, R. & Orion, R. (1990). When pupils do not understand the determinants of their success and failure in school: Relations between internal, teacher, and unknown perceptions of control and school achievement. *British Journal of Educational Psychology, 60,* 63–75.

176. Skinner, E. A., Wellborn, J. G. & Connell, J. P. (1990). What it takes to do well in school and whether I've got it: A process model of perceived control

and children's engagement and achievement in school. *Journal of Educational Psychology, 82,* 22–32.

177. Keith, T. Z. (1985). Effects of self-concept and locus of control on achievement. *Proceedings of the Annual Meeting of the National Association of School Psychologists,* Las Vegas: NV.

178. Shore, D. & Young, T. (1984). Locus of control: Ethnicity, SES, and academic achievement. *Proceedings of the Annual Meeting of the Educational Research Association,* New Orleans: LA.

179. Findley, M. J. & Cooper, H. M. (1983). Locus of control and academic achievement: A literature review. *Journal of Personality and Social Psychology, 44,* 419–427.

180. Coleman, J. S., Campbell, E. G., Hobsom, C. J., McPartland, J., Alexander, M., Weinfield, F. D. & York, R. L. (1966). *Equality of education opportunity.* Washington, D.C.: Department of Health, Education and Welfare.

181. Crandall, V. C., Katkovsky, W. & Crandall, F. J. (1965). Children's belief in their own control of reinforcements in intellectual-academic achievement situations. *Child Development, 36,* 91–109.

182. McGhee, P. E. & Crandall, V. C. (1968). Beliefs in internal-external control of reinforcements and academic performance. *Child Development, 39,* 132–149.

183. Nowicki, S. & Walker, C. (1973). The role of generalized and specific expectancies in determining academic achievement. *Journal of Social Psychology, 123,* 63–67.

184. Jones, E. (2008). Predicting performance in first-semester college basic writers: Revisiting the role of self–beliefs. *Contemporary Educational Psychology, 33,* 209–238.

185. Kirkpatrick, M. A., Stant, K., Downes, S. & Gaither, L. (2008). Perceived locus of control and academic performance: Broadening the construct's applicability. *Journal of College Student Development, 49,* 486–496.

186. Gifford, D. D., Briceno-Perriott, J. & Mianzo, F. (2006). Locus of control: Academic achievement and retention in a sample of university first-year students. *Journal of College Admissions, 191,* 18–25.

187. Shepherd, S., Fitch, T. J., Owen, D. & Marshal, J. L. (2006). Locus of control and academic achievement in high school students. *Psychology Reports, 98,* 318–322.

188. Linder, F. & Janus, C. E. (1997). The relationship of locus of control to academic performance among dental students. *Proceedings of the Annual Meeting of the Eastern Educational Research Association,* Hilton Head: SC.

189. Shell, D. F., Colvin, C. & Brunning, R. H. (1995). Self-efficacy, attribution, and outcome expectancy mechanisms in reading and writing achievement: Grade level and achievement-level differences. *Journal of Educational Psychology, 87,* 386–398.

190. Skinner, E. A., Wellborn, J. G. & Connell, J. P. (1990). What it takes to do well in school and whether I've got it: A process model of perceived control and children's engagement and achievement in school. *Journal of Educational Psychology, 82,* 22–32.

191. Crandall, V. C., Katkovsky, W. & Crandall, F. J. (1965). Children's belief in their own control of reinforcements in intellectual-academic achievement situations.

Child Development, 36, 91–109.

192. McGhee, P. E. & Crandall, V. C. (1968). Beliefs in internal-external control of reinforcements and academic performance. *Child Development, 39,* 132–149.

193. Nowicki, S. & Roundtree, J. (1971). Correlates of locus of control in secondary school age students. *Developmental Psychology, 4,* 479.

194. Powell, A. (1971). Alternative measures of locus of control and the prediction of academic performance. *Psychological Reports, 29,* 47–50.

195. Butterfield, E. C. (1964). Locus of control, test anxiety, reactions to frustration, and achievement attitudes. *Journal of Personality, 32,* 355–370.

196. McGhee, P. E. & Crandall, V. C. (1968). Beliefs in internal-external control of reinforcements and academic performance. *Child Development, 39,* 132–149.

197. Crandall, V. C., Katkovsky, W. & Crandall, F. J. (1965). Children's belief in their own control of reinforcements in intellectual-academic achievement situations. *Child Development, 36,* 91–109.

198. Massari, D. J. & Rosenblum, D. C. (1972). Locus of control, interpersonal trust and academic achievement. *Psychological Reports, 31,* 355–360.

199. McGhee, P. E. & Crandall, V. C. (1968). Beliefs in internal-external control of reinforcements and academic performance. *Child Development, 39,* 132–149.

200. Nowicki, S. & Roundtree, J. (1971). Correlates of locus of control in secondary school age students. *Developmental Psychology, 4,* 479.

201. Butterfield, E. C. (1964). Locus of control, test anxiety, reactions to frustration, and achievement attitudes. *Journal of Personality, 32,* 355–370.

202. Hall, C., Smith, K. & Chia, R. (2008). Cognitive and personality factors in relation to timely completion of a college degree. *College Student Journal, 42,* 1087–1098.

203. Landrum, R. E. (2010). Intent to apply to graduate school: Perceptions of senior year psychology majors. *North American Journal of Psychology, 12,* 243–254.

204. Sciarra, D. T. & Whitson, M. L. (2007). Predictive factors in postsecondary educational attainment among Latinos. *Professional School Counseling, 10,* 1096–2409.

205. Flouri, E. (2006). Parental interest in children's education, children's self-esteem and locus of control, and later educational attainment: Twenty-six year follow-up of the 1970 British Birth Cohort. *British Journal of Educational Psychology, 76,* 41–55.

206. Hawkes, B. B. (1995). Locus if control in early childhood education: Where did we come from? Where are we now? Where might we go from here? *Proceedings from the Annual Conference of the Midsouth Educational Research Association,* Biloxi: MS.

207. Dille, B. & Mezack, M. (1991). Identifying predictors of high risk among community college telecourse students. *American Journal of Distance Education, 8,* 22–39.

208. Yukselturk, E. & Bulut, S. (2007). Predictors for student success in an online course. *Educational Technology & Society, 10,* 71–83.

209. Burden, R. (2008). Is dyslexia necessarily associated with negative feelings of self-worth? A review and implications for further research. *Dyslexia, 14,*188–196.

210. Wojciszke, B. & Struzynska-Kujalowicz, A. (2007). Power influences self-esteem. *Social Cognition, 25,* 472–494.

211. McCullough, P. M. (1994). The effect of self-esteem, family structure, locus of control, and career goals on adolescent leadership behavior. *Adolescence, 29,* 605–611

212. Bobbitt, R. A. (1966). Internal-external control and bargaining behavior in a prisoner's dilemma game. (Unpublished doctoral dissertation). University of Texas, TX.

213. Guvenc, G. & Aktas, V. (2006). Age, gender, prejudice, interpersonal sensitivity and locus of control as predicters of self-esteem, assertiveness and communication skills in adolescents. *Turk Psikoloji Dergisi, 21,* 45–62.

214. Cooley, E. L. & Nowicki Jr., S. (1984). Locus of control and assertiveness in male and female college students. *Journal of Psychology, 117,* 85–87.

215. Hersch, P. D. & Scheibe, K. E. (1967). Reliability and validity of internal-external control as a personality dimension. *Journal of Consulting Psychology, 31,* 609–613.

216. Wojciszke, B. & Struzynska-Kujalowicz, A. (2007). Power influences self-esteem. *Social Cognition, 25,* 472–494.

217. Nowicki, S. & Roundtree, J. (1971). Correlates of locus of control in secondary school age students. *Developmental Psychology, 4,* 479.

218. Jones, S. C. & Shrauger, J. S. (1968). Locus of control and interpersonal evaluations. *Journal of consulting and Clinical Psychology, 32,* 664–668.

219. Wojciszke, B. & Struzynska-Kujalowicz, A. (2007). Power influences self-esteem. *Social Cognition, 25,* 472–494.

220. Adalbjarnardottir, S. (1995). How school children propose to negotiate: The role of social withdrawal, social anxiety and locus of control. *Child Development, 66,* 1739–1751.

221. Hersch, P. D. & Scheibe, K. E. (1967). Reliability and validity of internal-external control as a personality dimension. *Journal of Consulting Psychology, 31,* 609–613.

222. Phares, E. J. (1965). Internal-external control as a determinant of amount of social influence exerted. *Journal of Personality and Social Psychology, 2,* 642–647.

223. Gallagher, K. E. & Parrott, D. J. (2010). Influence of heavy episodic drinking on the relationship between men's locus of control and aggression towards intimate partners. *Journal of Studies on Alcohol and Drugs, 71,* 299–306.

224. Deming, A. M. & Lochman, J. E. (2008). The relation of locus of control anger, and impulsivity in boys' aggressive behavior. *Behavioral Disorders, 33,* 108–119.

225. Osterman, K., Bjorkqvist, K., Lagerspetz, K. M. J., Charpentier, S., Caprara, G. V. & Pastorelli, C. (1999). Locus of control and three types of aggression. *Aggressive Behavior, 25,* 61–65.

226. Avtgis, T. A. & Rancer, A. S. (1997). Argumentativeness and verbal aggressiveness as a function of locus of control. *Communication Research Reports, 14,* 441–450.

227. Rodriguez, C. M. (2010). Personal contextual characteristics and cognitions: Predicting child abuse potential and disciplinary style. *Journal of Interpersonal Violence, 25,* 315–355.

228. Osterman, K., Bjorkqvist, K., Lagerspetz, K. M. J., Charpentier, S., Caprara, G. V. & Pastorelli, C. (1999). Locus of control and three types of aggression. *Aggressive*

Behavior, 25, 61–65.

229. Davis, G. H. & Mettee, D. R. (1971). Internal versus external locus of control and magnitude of aggression toward self and others. *Psychological Reports, 29,* 403–411.

230. Goodstadt, B. E. & Hjelle, J. A. (1973). Power to the powerless: Locus of control and the use of power. *Journal of Personality and Social Psychology, 27,* 190–196.

231. Bierhoff, H. W., Klein, R. & Kramp, P. (2006). Evidence for the altruistic personality from data on accident research. *Journal of Personality, 59,* 263–280.

232. Bradley, R. H. & Teeter, T. A. (2006). Perceptions of control over social outcomes and student behavior. *Psychology in the Schools, 14,* 230–235.

233. Midlarsky, E., Fagen, J. S. & Corley, R. P. (2005). Personality correlates heroic rescue during the Holocaust. *Journal of Personality, 73,* 907–934.

234. Campbell, K. & de Man, A. F. (2000). Threat perception and reluctance to donate organs. *North American Journal of Psychology, 2,* 21–26.

235. Midlarsky, E. (1971). Aiding under stress: The effects of competence, dependency, visibility, and fatalism. *Journal of Personality, 39,* 132–149.

236. Liu, X., Kurita, H., Uchiyama, M., Okawa, M., Liu, L. & Ma, D. (2000). Life events, locus of control, and behavioral problems among Chinese adolescents. *Journal of Clinical Psychology, 56,* 1565–1577.

237. Trice, A. D. (1990). Adolescents' locus of control and compliance with contingency contracting and counseling interventions. *Psychological Reports, 67.* 233–234.

238. Masi, W. S. (1972). Antecedents and correlates of locus of control in high school students.

239. Brissett, M. & Nowicki, S. (1973). Internal versus external control of reinforcement and reaction to frustration. *Journal of Personality and Social Psychology, 25,* 35–44.

240. Butterfield, E. C. (1964). Locus of control, test anxiety, reactions to frustration, and achievement attitudes. *Journal of Personality, 32,* 355–370.

241. Aremu, A. O., Pakes, F. & Johnston, L. (2009). The effects of locus of control in the reduction of corruption in Nigerian police. *Policing, 32,* 144–156.

242. Ceyhan, A. A. & Ceyhan, E. (2007). The relationships among unethical usage behavior and some personality characteristics of Turkish university students. *Proceedings from the International Educational Technology (IETC) Conference,* Nicosia: Turkish Republic of Northern Cypress.

243. Manley, G. G., Benavidez, J. & Dunn, K. (2007). Development of a personality biodata measure to predict ethical decision making. *Journal of Managerial Psychology, 22,* 664–682.

244. Trevino, L. K. & Youngblood, S. A. (1990). Bad apples in bad barrels: A causal analysis of ethical decision-making behavior. *Journal of Applied Psychology, 75,* 378–385.

245. Visher, S. (1986). The relationship of locus of control and contraceptive use in the adolescent population. *Journal of Adolescent Health Care, 7,* 183–186.

246. Young, T. M., Martin, S. S., Young, M. E. & Ting, L. (2001). Internal poverty and teen pregnancy. *Adolescence, 36,* 289–304.

247. Morgan, C. & Chapar, G. N. (1995). Psychosocial variables associated with teenage pregnancy. *Adolescence, 30,* 277.

248. Tinsley, B. J., Trupin, S. R., Owens, L. & Boyum, L. A. (1993). The significance of women's pregnancy-related locus of control beliefs to adherence of recommended prenatal health regimens and pregnancy outcomes. *Journal of Reproductive and Infant Psychology, 11,* 97–102.

249. Zycinska, J. (2009). The role of beliefs and expectations in adopting health behaviors by pregnant smokers. *European Psychiatry, 24,* 478.

250. Goodman, W., Leggett, J. & Garrett, T. (2007). Locus of control in offenders and alleged offenders with learning disabilities. *British Journal of Learning Disabilities, 35,* 192–197.

251. Gaum, G., Hoffmann, S. & Venter, J. H. (2006). Factors that influence adult recidivism: An exploratory study in Pollsmoor prison. *South African Journal of Psychology, 36,* 407–424.

252. Aremu, A. O., Pakes, F. & Johnston, L. (2009). The effects of locus of control in the reduction of corruption in Nigerian police. *Policing, 32,* 144–156.

253. Trice, A. D. (1990). Adolescents' locus of control and compliance with contingency contracting and counseling interventions. *Psychological Reports, 67.* 233–234.

254. Johnson, T. B. (1969). An examination of some relationships between anomie and selected personality and sociological correlates in a sample of high school dropouts. (Unpublished doctoral dissertation). University of California, Berkley.

255. Seeman, M. (1967). On the personal consequences of alienation in work. *American Sociological Review, 32,* 273–285

256. Clouser, R. A. & Hjelle, L. A. (1970). Relationship between locus of control and dogmatism. *Psychological Reports, 26,* 1006.

257. Seeman, M. (1967). On the personal consequences of alienation in work. *American Sociological Review, 32,* 273–285.

258. Seeman, M. (1967). Powerlessness and knowledge: A comparative study of alienation and learning. *Sociometry, 30,* 105–123.

259. Alp, E., Ertepinar, H., Tekkaya, C. & Yilmaz, A. (2008). A survey on Turkish elementary school students' environmentally friendly behaviors and associated variables. *Environmental Education Research, 14,* 129–143.

260. Strickland, B. R. (1965). The prediction of social action from a dimension of internal-external control. *Journal of Social Psychology, 66,* 353–358.

261. Hotchkiss, L. (1984). *Post high school labor market outcomes and schooling.* Paper Presented at the Annual Meeting of the American Educational Research Associations, San Francisco, CA.

262. Cebi, M. (2007). Locus of control and human capital investment revisited. *Journal of Human Resources, 52,* 919–932.

263. Grable, J. E., Joo-Yung, P. & So-Hyun, J. (2009). Explaining financial management behavior for Koreans living in the United States. *Journal of Consumer Affairs, 43,* 80–107.

264. Judge, T. A. (2009). Core self-evaluations and work success. *Current Directions in Psychological Science, 18,* 58–62.

265. Fogarty, G. J. & McGrogor-Bayne, H. (2008). Factors that influence career decision-making among elite athletes. *Australian Journal of Career Development, 17,* 26–38.

266. Huang, H. (2006). Understanding culinary art workers: Locus of control, job satisfaction, work stress, and turnover intention. *Journal of Foodservice Business Research, 9,* 151–168.

267. Judge, T. A. (2009). Core self-evaluations and work success. *Current Directions in Psychological Science, 18,* 58–62.

268. Hansson, H. (2008). How can farmer managerial capacity contribute to improved farm performance? A study of dairy farms in Sweden. *Acta Agricultural Scandinavica: Section C – Food Economics, 5,* 44–61.

269. Erez, A. & Judge. T. A. (2001). Relationship of core self-evaluations to goal-setting, motivation, and performance. *Journal of Applied Psychology, 86,* 1270–1279.

270. Judge, T. A. & Bono, J. E. (2001). Relationship of core self-evaluations traits—self esteem, generalized self-efficacy, locus of control and emotional stability—with job satisfaction and job performance: A meta-analysis.

271. Mudrack, P. E. (1990). Machiavellianism and locus of control: A meta-analytic review. *Journal of Social Psychology, 130,* 125–126.

272. Bazylewicz-Walczak, B. (1985). Individualistic determinants of work reliability in operators of automated production processes. *Polish Psychological Bulletin, 16,* 181–189.

273. Michon, H. W., ten Have, M., Kroon, H., van Weeghel, J., de Graaf, R. & Schene, A. H. (2008). Mental disorders and personality traits as determinants of impaired work functioning. *Psychological Medicine, 38,* 1627–1637.

274. Krenl, L. (1992). The moderating effects of locus of control on performance incentives and paticipation. *Human Relations, 45,* 991–1012.

275. Elkind, P. D. (2007). Perceptions of risk, stressors, and locus of control influence intentions to practice safety behaviors in agriculture. *Journal of Agromedicine, 12,* 7–25.

276. Cigularov, K. P., Chen, P. Y. & Stallones, L. (2009). Error communication in young farm workers: Its relationship to safety climate and safety locus of control. *Work and Stress, 23,* 297–312.

277. Hansson, H. (2008). How can farmer managerial capacity contribute to improved farm performance? A study of dairy farms in Sweden. *Acta Agricultural Scandinavica: Section C – Food Economics, 5,* 44–61.

278. Judge, T. A. (2009). Core self-evaluations and work success. *Current Directions in Psychological Science, 18,* 58–62.

279. Keller, J. & Blomann, F. (2008). Locus of control and the flow experience: An experimental analysis. *European Journal of Personality, 22,* 589–607.

280. Mudrack, P. E. (1990). Machiavellianism and locus of control: A meta-analytic review. *Journal of Social Psychology, 130,* 125–126.

281. Selander, J., Marnetoft, S. & Asell, M. (2007). Predictors for successful vocational rehabilitation for clients with back pain problems. *Disability and Rehabilitation, 29,* 215–220.

282. Nickasch, B & Marnocha, S. K. (2009). Healthcare experiences of the homeless. *Journal of the American Academy of Nurse Practitioners, 21*, 39–46.

283. McDonnall, M. C. & Crudden, A. (2009). Factors affecting the successful employment of transition-age youths with visual impairments. *Journal of Visual Impairment & Blindness, 103*,329–341.

284. Becker, B. E. & Hills, S. M. (1979). Teenage locus of control and adult unemployment. Department of Labor, Washington, D.C.

285. Watson, D. (1967). Relationship between locus of control and anxiety. *Journal of Personality and Social Psychology, 6*, 91–92.

286. Tokunaga, H. (1993). The use and abuse of consumer credit: Application of psychological theory and research. *Journal of Economic Psychology, 14*, 285–316.

287. Bruk-Lee, V., Khoury, H. A., Nixon, A. E., Goh, A. & Spector, P. E. (2009). Replicating and extending past personality/ job satisfaction meta-analysis. *Human Performance, 22*, 156–189.

288. Judge, T. A. (2009). Core self-evaluations and work success. *Current Directions in Psychological Science, 18, 58–62.*

289. Kass-Shraibman, F. (2008). An examination of the job satisfaction of certified public accountants as it related to their area of practice and their locus of control. *Dissertation Abstracts International Section A: Humanities and Social Sciences, 69,* 855.

290. Bein, J., Anderson, D. E. & Maes, W. R. (1990). Teacher locus of control and job satisfaction. *Educational Research Quarterly, 14, 7–10.*

291. Ng, T. W. H., Sorensen, K. L. & Eby, L. T. (2006). Locus of control at work: A meta-analysis. *Journal of Organizational Behavior, 27,* 1057–1087.

292. Judge, T. A. & Bono, J. E. (2001). Relationship of core self-evaluations traits— self-esteem, generalized self-efficacy, locus of control and emotional stability— with job satisfaction and job performance: A meta-analysis.

293. Spector, P. E. (1982). Behavior in organizations as a function of employee's locus of control. *Psychological Bulletin, 91,* 482–497.

294. Reimers-Hild, C. (2007). "Entrepreneurial" qualities help online learners succeed. *Online Classroom,* 2–5.

295. Hansemark, O. C. (2003). Need for achievement, locus of control and the prediction of business start-ups: A longitudinal study. *Journal of Economic Psychology, 24,* 301–319.

296. Kaufmann, P.J., Welsh, D.H.B., & Bushmarin, N. (1995). Locus of control and entrepreneurship in the Russian Republic. *Entrepreneurship Theory and Practice, 20,* 43–56.

297. Miller, D., Kets de Vries, M. F. R. & Toulouse, J. (1982). Top executive locus of control and its relationship to strategy-making, structure, and environment. *Academy of Management Journal, 25,* 237–253.

298. Heineck, G. & Anger, S. (2010). The returns to cognitive abilities and personality traits in Germany. *Labour Economics, 17,* 535–546.

299. Groves, M. O. (2005). How important is you personality? Labor market returns to personality for women in the US and UK. *Journal of Economic Psychology, 26,* 827–841.

300. Goldsmith, A. H., Veum, J. R. & Darity, W. (1997). The Impact of Psychological and Human Capital on Wages. *Economic Inquiry 35*, 815–29.
301. Frantz, R. (1982). Attitudes and work performance among young men during the transition from school to work. *American Economist, 26.*
302. Frantz, R. S. (1980). Internal-external locus of control and labor market performance: Empirical evidence using longitudinal survey data. *Psychology: A Quarterly Journal of Human Behavior, 17,* 23–29.
303. Frantz, R. (1982). Attitudes and work performance among young men during the transition from school to work. *American Economist, 26.*
304. Nickasch, B & Marnocha, S. K. (2009). Healthcare experiences of the homeless. *Journal of the American Academy of Nurse Practitioners, 21,* 39–46.
305. Gardner, D. (2007). Confronting the achievement gap. *Phi Delta Kappan, 88,* 542–546.
306. Stephens, M. W. & Delys, P. (1973). External control expectancies among disadvantaged children at preschool age. *Child Development, 44,* 670–674.
307. Gale, C. R., Battty, D. & Deary, I. J. (2008). Locus of control at age 10 years and health outcomes and behaviors at age 30 years: The 1970 British cohort study. *Psychosomatic Medicine, 70,* 379–403.
308. Gilhooly, M., Hanlon, P., Cullen, B., Macdonals, S. & Whyte, B. (2007). Successful ageing in an area of deprivation: Part 2 – A quantitative exploration of the role of personality and beliefs in good health in old age. *Public Health, 121,* 814–821.
309. Lee, S. (2003). Health behaviors in people with serious mental illness: The role of illness cognition, optimism, and health locus of control of diabetes. *Dissertation Abstracts International: Section B: The Sciences and Engineering, 64,* 2926.
310. Korkeila, J. (2000). *Measuring aspects of mental health.* National Research and Development Centre for Welfare and Health, Helsinki.
311. Evans, J. H. (1991). The relationship between internal locus of control and rehabilitation prognosis.
312. Berg, A. I., Hoffman, L., Bjork, L., McClearn, G. E. Johansson, B. (2009). What matters and what matters most, for change in life satisfaction in the oldest-old? A study over 6 years among individuals 80+. *Aging and Mental Health, 13,* 191–201.
313. Radant, F., Lanteri-Minet, M., Nachit-Ouinekh, F., Massiou, H., Lucas, C., Pradalier, A., Mercier, F. & El Hasnaoui, A. (2009). The GRIM2005 study of migraine consultation in France. III : Psychological features of subjects with migraine. *Cephalalgia, 29,* 338–350.
314. Gale, C. R., Battty, D. & Deary, I. J. (2008). Locus of control at age 10 years and health outcomes and behaviors at age 30 years: The 1970 British cohort study. *Psychosomatic Medicine, 70,* 379–403.
315. Ali, S. M. & Lindstrom, M. (2006). Socioeconomic, pychosocial, behavioural, and psychological determinants of BMI among young women: Differing patterns for underweight and overweight/obesity. *European Journal of Public Health, 16,* 325–331.
316. Gale, C. R., Battty, D. & Deary, I. J. (2008). Locus of control at age 10 years and health outcomes and behaviors at age 30 years: The 1970 British cohort study. *Psychosomatic Medicine, 70,* 379–403.

317. Nowack, K. M. & Sassenrath, J. M. (1980). Coronary-prone behavior, locus of control, and anxiety. *Psychological Reports, 47,* 359–364.

318. Pruessner, J. C., Baldwin, J. W., Dedovic, K., Renwick, R., Mahani, N. K., Lord, C., Meaney, M. & Lupien, S. (2005). Self-esteem, locus of control, hippocampal volume and cortisol regulation in young and old adulthood. *NeuroImage, 28,* 815–826.

319. Zycinska, J. (2009). The role of beliefs and expectations in adopting health behaviors by pregnant smokers. *European Psychiatry, 24,* 478.

320. Park, C. L. & Gaffey, A. E. (2007). Relationships between psychosocial factors and health behavior change in cancer survivors: An integrative review. *Annals of Behavioral Medicine, 34,* 115–134.

321. Wallhagen, M. I. (1994). Impact of internal health locus of control on health outcomes for older men and women: A longitudinal perspective. *Gerontologist, 34,* 299–306.

322. Weiss, G. L. & Larsen, D. L. (1990). Health value, health locus of control, and the prediction of health protective behaviors. *Social Behavior & Personality, 18,* 121–135.

323. Thomas, S. P. (1984). Predictors of health in middle adulthood. *Proceedings of the Annual Convention of the American Psychological Association,* Toronto ON: Canada.

324. Wallston, B. S. & Wallston, K. A. (1978). Locus of control and health: A review of the literature. *Health Education Monographs, 6,* 107–117.

325. Strickland, B. R. (1973). Locus of control: Where have we been and where are we going? *Proceedings from the Annual Meeting of the American Psychological Association,* Montreal: Canada.

326. Mei-Yu, Y. (2008). Measuring readiness to change and locus of control belief among male alcohol-dependent patients is Taiwan: Comparison of the different degrees of alcohol dependence. *Psychiatry and Clinical Neuroscience, 62,* 533–539.

327. Thurman, P. J., Jones-Saumty, D. & Parsons, O. A. (1990). Locus of control and drinking behavior in American Indian alcoholics and non-alcoholics. *American Indian and Alaska Native Mental Health Research, 4,* 31–39.

328. Booth-Butterfield, M., Anderson, R. H. & Booth-Butterfield, S. (2000). Adolescents' use of tobacco, health locus of control and self-monitoring. *Health Communication, 12,* 137–148.

329. Segall, M. E. & Wynd, C. A. (1990). Health conception, health locus of control, and power as predictors of smoking behavior change. *American Journal of Health Promotion, 4,* 338–344.

330. Wallston, B. S. & Wallston, K. A. (1978). Locus of control and health: A review of the literature. *Health Education Monographs, 6,* 107–117.

331. Aberle, I., Scholz, U., Bach-Kliegel, B., Fischer, C., Gorney, M., Langer, K. & Kliegel, M. (2009). Psychological aspects in continuous subcutaneous insulin infusion: A retrospective study. *Journal of Psychology, 143,* 147–160.

332. Gordijn, E. H. & Boven, G. (2009). Loneliness among people with HIV in relation to locus of control and negative meta-stereotyping. *Basic and Applied*

Social Psychology, 31, 109–116.

333. Mitsonis, C., Potagas, C., Zervas, I. & Sfagos, K. (2009). The effects of stressful life events on the course of multiple sclerosis: A review. *International Journal of Neuroscience, 119,* 315–335.

334. Reinhardt, J. P., Boerner, K. & Horowitz, A. (2009). Personal and social resources and adaptation to chronic vision impairment over time. *Aging and Mental Health, 13,* 367–375.

335. Heath, R. L., Saliba, M., Mahmassani, O., Major, S. C. & Khoury, B. A. (2008). Locus of control moderates the relationship between headache pain and depression. *Journal of Headache and Pain, 9,* 301–308.

336. Izaute, M., Durozard, C., Aldigier, E., Teissedre, F., Perreve, A. & Gerbaud, L. (2008). Perceived social support and locus of control after traumatic brain injury (TBI). *Brain Injury, 22,* 758–764.

337. Moore, S. M., Prior, K. N. & Bond, M. J. (2007). The contributions of psychological disposition and risk factor status to health following treatment for coronary artery disease. *European Journal of Cardiovascular Nursing, 6,* 137–145.

338. Neipp, M., Lopez-Roig, S. & Pastor, M. A. (2007). Control beliefs in cancer: A review of the literature. *Anuario de Psicologia, 38,* 333–355.

339. Sagduyu, A., Senturk, V. H., Sezer, S., Emiroglu, R. & Ozel, S. (2006). Psychiatric problems, life quality and compliance in patients treated with haemodialysis and renal transplantation. *Turkish Journal of Psychiatry, 17,* 22–31.

340. Watson, M., Greer, S., Pruyn, J. & Van der Norne, B. (1990). Locus of control and adjustment to cancer. *Psychological Reports, 66,* 39–48.

341. Aberle, I., Scholz, U., Bach-Kliegel, B., Fischer, C., Gorney, M., Langer, K. & Kliegel, M. (2009) Psychological aspects in continuous subcutaneous insulin infusion: A retrospective study. *Journal of Psychology, 143,* 147–160.

342. Mitsonis, C., Potagas, C., Zervas, I. & Sfagos, K. (2009). The effects of stressful life events on the course of multiple sclerosis: A review. *International Journal of Neuroscience, 119,* 315–335.

343. Sturmer, T., Hasselbach, P. & Amelang, M. (2006). Personality, lifestyle, and risk of cardiovascular disease and cancer: Follow-up of population based cohort. *British Medical Journal, 332,* 1359–1362.

344. Nusselder, W. J., Looman, C. W. N & Mackenbach, J. P. (2005). Nondisease factors affected trajectories of disability in a prospective study. *Journal of Clinical Epidemiology, 58,* 484–494.

345. Hong, T., Oddone, E., Dudley, T. K. & Bosworth, H. B. (2006). Medication barriers and anti-hypertensive medication adherence: The moderating role of locus of control. *Psychology, Health and Medicine, 11,* 20–28.

346. Middleton, A. (2004). Chronic low back pain: Patient compliance with physiotherapy advice and exercise, perceived barriers and motivation. *Physical Therapy Reviews, 9,* 153–160.

347. Torres, X., Collado, A., Arias, A., Peri, J. M., Bailles, E., Salamero, M. & Valdes, M. (2009). Pain locus of control predicts return to work among Spanish fibromyalgia patterns after completion of a multidisiplinary pain program. *General Hospital Psychiatry, 31,* 137–145.

348. Gillibrand, R. & Stevenson, J. (2006). The extended health belief model applied to the experience of diabetes in young people. *British Journal of Health Psychology, 11,* 155–169.

349. Evans, J. H. (1991). The relationship between internal locus of control and rehabilitation prognosis.

350. Hudzinski, L. G. & Levenson, H. (1985). Biofeedback behavioral treatment of headache with locus of control pain analysis: A 20-month restrospective study. *Headache: The Journal of Head and Face Pain, 25,* 380–386.

351. Van Oort, F. V. A., van Lenthe, F. J. & Mackenbach, J. P. (2005). Material, psychosocial, and behavioral factors in the explanation of educational inequalities in mortality in the Netherlands. *Journal of Epidemiological and Community Health, 59,* 214–220.

352. Krause, N. & Shaw, B. A. (2000). Role-specific feelings of control and mortality. *Psychology and Aging, 15,* 617–626.

353. Bosma, H., Schrijvers, C. & Mackenbach, J. P. (1999). Socioeconomic inequalities in mortality and importance of perceived control: Cohort study. *BMJ, 319,* 1469–1470.

354. Dalgard, O. S. & Haheim, L. L. (1998). Psychosocial risk factors and mortality: A prospective study with special focus of social support, social participation and locus of control in Norway. *Journal of Epidemiology and Community Health, 52,* 476–481.

355. Armstrong, M. I. & Boothroyd, R. A. (2008). Predictors of emotional well-being in at-risk adolescent girls: Developing preventative intervention strategies. *Journal of Behavioral Health Services & Research, 35,* 435–453.

356. Hill, E. D., Terrell, H. K., Hladkyj, S. & Nagoshi, C. T. (2009). Validation of the Narrative Emplotment Scale and its correlations with well-being and psychological adjustment. *British Journal of Psychology, 100,* 675–698.

357. Judge, T. A. (2009). Core self-evaluations and work success. *Current Directions in Psychological Science, 18,* 58–62.

358. Sagduyu, A., Senturk, V. H., Sezer, S., Emiroglu, R. & Ozel, S. (2006). Psychiatric problems, life quality and compliance in patients treated with haemodialysis and renal transplantation. *Turkish Journal of Psychiatry, 17,* 22–31.

359. Branholm, I., Fugl-Meyer, A. R. & Frolunde, A. (1998). Life satisfaction, sense of coherence and locus of control in occupational therapy students. *Scandinavian Journal of Occupational Therapy, 5,* 39–44.

360. Lewis, V. G & Borders, L. D. (1995). Life satisfaction of single middle-aged professional women. *Journal of Counseling and Development, 74,* 94–100.

361. Ryff, C. D. (1989). Happiness is everything, or is it? Explorations on the meaning of psychological well-being. *Journal of Personality and Social Psychology, 57,* 1069–1081.

362. Warehime, R. G. & Foulds, M. F. (1971). Perceived locus of control and personal adjustment. *Journal of Consulting and Clinical Psychology, 37,* 250–252.

363. Heady, BB. (2008). Life goals matter to happiness: A revision of set-point theory. *Social Indicators Research, 86,* 213–231.

364. Christopher, A. N., Saliba, L. & Deadmarsh, E. J. (2009). Materialism and

well-being: The mediating effect of locus of control. *Personality and Individual Differences, 46,* 682–686.

365. Verme, P. (2009). Happiness, freedom and control. *Journal of Economic Behavior & Organization, 71,* 146–161.

366. Kelly, T. M. & Stack, S. A. (2000). Thought recognition, locus of control, and adolescent well-being. *Adolescence.*

367. Branholm, I., Fugl-Meyer, A. R. & Frolunde, A. (1998). Life satisfaction, sense of coherence and locus of control in occupational therapy students. *Scandinavian Journal of Occupational Therapy, 5,* 39–44.

368. Kopp, R. G. & Ruzicka, M. F. (1993). Women's multiple roles and psychological well-being. *Psychological Reports, 72,* 1351–1355.

369. Reid, D. W., Haas, G. & Hawkings, D. (1977). Locus of desired control and positive self concept in elderly. *The Gerontological Society of America, 32,* 441–450.

370. Knapp, S. & Pinquart, M. (2009). Tracing criteria of successful aging? Health locus of control and well-being in older patients with internal disease. *Psychology, Health and Medicine, 14,* 201–212.

371. Knapp, S. & Pinquart, M. (2009). Tracing criteria of successful aging? Health locus of control and well-being in older patients with internal disease. *Psychology, Health and Medicine, 14,* 201–212. ∎

372. Reid, D. W., Haas, G. & Hawkings, D. (1977). Locus of desired control and positive self concept in elderly. *The Gerontological Society of America, 32,* 441–450.

373. Cherry, J. (2006). The impact of normative influence and locus of control on ethical judgments and intentions: A cross cultural comparison. *Journal of Business Ethics, 68,* 113–132.

374. Kulshreshtha, U. & Kashyap, R. (2004). Psychological correlates of clothing conformity among adolescents. *Journal of the Indian Academy of Applied Psychology, 30,* 21–27.

375. Forte, A. (2005). Locus of control and the moral reasoning of managers. *Journal of Business Ethics, 58,* 65–77.

376. Biondo, J. & MacDonald, A. P. (1971). Internal-external locus of control and response to influence attempts. *Journal of Personality, 39,* 407–419.

377. Gozali, J. & Sloan, J. (1971). Reflections on the categorization of human excellence. *The Journal of Psychology, 31,* 207–211.

378. Albert, D. F. (2008). Embraced by hope: The resilience of former Latino gang members (California). *Dissertation Abstracts International Section A: Humanities and Social Sciences, 68,* 3608.

379. Cole, C. A. & Singh, S. (1985). The effect of locus of control on message acceptance and recall. *Proceedings from the Annual Convention of the American Psychological Association,* Los Angeles: CA.

380. Bloomberg, M. & Soneson, S. (1976). The effect of locus of control and field independence-dependence on moral reasoning. *Journal of Genetic Psychology, 128,* 59–67.

381. Garson, B. E. & Stanwyke, D. J. (1997). Locus of control and incentive in self-

managing teams. *Human Resources Quarterly Development,8,* 247–258.

382. Reynolds, S. J. & Ceranic, T. L. (2009). *On the causes and conditions of moral behavior: Why is this all we know?* In Psychological perspectives of ethical behavior and decision making. David de Cremer (Ed.) Information Age Publishing, 17–33.

383. Gutkin, D. C. & Suls, J. (1979). The relation between the ethics of personal conscience-social responsibility and principled moral reasoning. *Journal of Youth and Adolescence, 8,* 433–441.

384. Knoop, R. (1995). Encouraging individual responsibility: Why individuals feel powerless and the possible implications for education. *Education Canada, 35,* 40–42.

385. Dienstbier, R. A. (1975). Exposure to theories of conscience as a determinant of cheating.

386. Karabenick, S. A. & Srull, T. K. (1978). Effects of personality and situational variation in locus of control on cheating: Determinants of the "congruence effect". *Journal of Personality, 46,* 72–95.

387. National Assessment of Educational Progress. (2005). Americas charter schools. Results from the NAEP 2003 pilot study.

Chapter 3

1. Skuy, M. (1987) Use of the learning potential assessment device and remediation of a learning problem. *Proceedings from the Annual International Conference of the Association for Children and Adults with Learning Disabilities. San Antonio: TX.*

2. Camp, B. W. (1977). Verbal mediation in young aggressive boys. *Journal of Abnormal Psychology, 86,* 145–153.

3. Dush, D. M., Hirt, M. L. & Schroeder, H. E. (1989). Self-statement modification in treatment of of child behavior disorders: A meta analysis.*Psychological Bulletin, 1,* 97–106.

4. Harris, K. R. (1990). Developing self-regulated learners: The role of private speech and self instructions. *Educational Psychologist, 25,* 36–49.

5. Kendall, P. C. (1977). On the efficacious use of verbal self-instructional procedures with children. *Cognitive Therapy and Research, 1,* 331–341.

6. Skuy, M. (1987). Use of the learning potential assessment device and remediation of a learning problem. *Proceedings from the Annual International Conference of the Association for Children and Adults with Learning Disabilities. San Antonio: TX.*

7. Winsler, Fernyhough & Montero (Eds.). (2009). *Private speech, executive function and the development of verbal self-regulation.* New York, NY: Cambridge University Press.

8. Hill, R. A. & Campiglia, H. (1972). *ACT—Achievement Competence Training: A report, part V: Utilization of formative evaluation.* Philadelphia, Pa.; Research for Better Schools, Inc.

9. Fritson, K. K. (2008). Impact of journaling on students' self-efficacy and locus of

control. *InSight: A Journal of Scholarly Teaching, 3*, 75–80.

10. Kagan, J. & Moss, H. A. (1962). Birth to Maturity: A Study in Psychological Development. John Wiley and Sons Inc, Hobokin, N.J.

11. Lefcourt, H. M. (1982). Locus of control: Current trends in theory and research. (2nd edition). Hillsdale, NJ: Lawrence Erlbaum Associates, Publishers.

12. deCharms, R. (1976). Enhancing Motivation. New York, NY: Irvington Publishers Inc.

13. Raspberry, W. (2005). Poor woman's 'magical outlook'. *Washington Post*: September 26, 2005.

14. Hill, R. A. (1973). Teaching children to use achievement behaviors and dispositions for setting and achieving goals. Washington, DC: National Institute of Education.

15. Brownell, P. (1981). Participation in budgeting, locus of control and organizational effectiveness. *Dissertation Abstracts International, 40*, 4101–4102.

16. Kelly, D. F. (2002). The effect of locus of control, gender and grade upon children's preference for praise or encouragement. *Journal of Individual Psychology, 58*, 197–207.

Chapter 4

1. Davy, L. How a 5th grader thinks. Retrieved from http://www.education.com/magazine/article.How_child_thinks_fifth_graders/

2. Hill, R. A. (1972). The achievement competence training package of the humanizing learning program. *Research for Better Schools Inc.*

3. Bialer, I. (1961). Conceptualization of success and failure in mentally retarded and normative children. *Journal of Personality, 29*, 303–320.

4. Nowicki, S. & Barnes, J. (1973). Effects of a structured camp experience on locus of control orientation. *Journal of Genetic Psychology, 122*, 247–252.

5. Lifshitz, M. (1973). Internal-external locus-of-control dimension as a function of age and the socialization milieu. *Child Development, 44*, 538–546.

6. Reimanis, G. (1970). A study of home environment and readiness for achievement at school. Final report.

7. Pierce, R. M., Schauble, P. G. & Farkas, A. (1973). Teaching internalization behavior to clients. *Psychotherapy: Theory Research and Practice, 7*, 217–220.

8. Hill, R. A. (1972). The achievement competence training package of the humanizing learning program. *Research for Better Schools Inc.*

9. Hill, R. A. (1972). The achievement competence training package of the humanizing learning program. *Research for Better Schools Inc.*

10. Katz, I. (1968). Academic motivation and equal opportunity. *Harvard Educational Review, 38*, 57–65.

11. Enkin, M. W. & Jadad, A. R. (1998). Using anecdotal information in evidence-based health care: Heresy or necessary? *Annals of Oncology, 9*, 963–966.

12. Wittink, H., Nicholas, M., Kralik, D. & Verbunt, J. (2008). Are we measuring what we need to measure? *Clinical Journal of Pain, 24*, 316–324.

13. Hill, R. A. (1973). Teaching children to use achievement behaviors and

dispositions for setting and achieving goals. Washington, DC: National Institute of Education.

14. Hill, R. A. & Campiglia, H. (1972). *ACT—Achievement Competence Training: A report, part V: Utilization of formative evaluation.* Philadelphia, Pa.; Research for Better Schools, Inc.

15. Hill, R. A. (1973). Teaching children to use achievement behaviors and dispositions for setting and achieving goals. Washington, DC: National Institute of Education.

16. Wiesner, W. & Cronshaw, S. F. (1988). A meta-analytic investigation of the impact of interview format and degree of structure on the validity of the employment interview. *Journal of Occupational Psychology, 61,* 275–290.

Chapter 5

1. Cichoki, M. (2006). Universal Precautions. *Centers for Disease Control and Prevention.* Retrieved [12/17/2010] from http://aids.about.com/od/glossary/g/universal.htm

2. Hill, R. A. (1972). The achievement competence training package of the humanizing learning program. *Research for Better Schools Inc.*

3. Wang, Q. Bowling, N. A. & Eschleman, K. J. (2010). Wanted: Employees with high work locus of control. *Journal of Applied Psychology, 95,* 761–768.

4. Huang, H. (2006). Understanding culinary art workers: Locus of control, job satisfaction, work stress and turnover intention. *Journal of Foodservice Business Research, 9,* 151–168.

5. Judge, T. A. (2009). Core self-evaluations and work success. *Current Directions in Psychological Science, 18,* 58–62.

6. Keller, J. & Blomann, F. (2008). Locus of control and the flow experience: An experimental analysis. *European Journal of Personality, 22,* 589–607.

7. Kass-Shraibman, F. (2008). An examination of the job satisfaction of certified public accountants as it related to their area of practice and their locus of control. *Dissertation Abstracts International Section A: Humanities and Social Sciences, 69,* 855.

8. Fritson, K. K. (2008). Impact of journaling on students' self-efficacy and locus of control. *InSight: A Journal of Scholarly Teaching, 3,* 75–80.

Chapter 6

1. Hainline, L. & Feig, E. (1979). Correlates of childhood father absence in college-aged women. *Child Development, 49,* 37–42.

2. Parish, T.S. & Nunn, G. D. (1983) Locus of control as a function of family type and age of onset of father absence. *Journal of Psychology, 133,* 187–190.

3. Cohen, E., Sade, M., Benarroch, F., Pollak, Y. & Gross-Tsur, V. (2008). Locus of control, perceived parenting style and symptoms of anxiety and depression in children with Tourette's syndrome. *European Child and Adolescent Psychiatry, 17,* 299–305.

4. Suizzo, M. & Soon, K. (2006). Parental academic socialization: Effects of home-

based parental involvement on locus of control across U.S. ethnic groups. *Educational Psychology, 26,* 827–846.

5. Boldt, R. W., Witzel, M., Russell, C. & Jones, V. (2007). Replacing coercive power with relationship power. *Reclaiming Children and Youth: The Journal of Strength-based Interventions 15,* 243–248.

6. Boldt, R. W., Witzel, M., Russell, C. & Jones, V. (2007). Replacing coercive power with relationship power. *Reclaiming Children and Youth: The Journal of Strength-based Interventions 15,* 243–248.

7. Janssens, J. M. A. M. (1994). Authoritarian child rearing, parental locus of control, and the child's behavior style. *International Journal of Behavior Development, 17,* 485–501.

8. Battle, E. & Rotter, J. B. (1963). Children's feelings of personal control as related to social class and ethnic group. *Journal of Personality, 31,* 482–490.

9. Nickasch, B & Marnocha, S. K. (2009). Healthcare experiences of the homeless. *Journal of the American Academy of Nurse Practitioners, 21,* 39–46.

10. Borman, G. D. & Rachuba, L. T. (2001). *Academic success among poor and minority students: An analysis of competing models of school effects.* Center for Research on the Education of Students Placed at Risk, Baltimore, MD.

11. Angel, R. J., Angel, J. L. & Hill, T. D. (2009). Subjective control and health among Mexican-origin elders in Mexico and the United States: Structural considerations in comparative research. *Journals of Gerontology Series B: Psychological Sciences and Social Sciences, 64B,* 390–401.

12. Time management. Retrieved [12–08–2010] from http://en.wikipedia.org/wiki/Time_management.

13. Addictive personality disorder. Retrieved [12–08–2010] from http://lifestyle.iloveindia.com/lounge/addictive-personality-disorder-4500.html.

14. Nelson, B. (1983, January 18). The addictive personality: Common traits are found. *New York Times.* Retrieved from http://www.nytimes.com/983/01/18/science/the-addictive-personality-common-traits-are-found.html.

15. Goodship, J. M. (1990). Life skills mastery for students with special needs. *Eric Digests*

16. Vuger-Kovacic, D., Gregurek, R., Kovacic, D., Vuger, T. & Kalenic, B. (2007). Relation between anxiety, depression and locus of control of patients with multiple sclerosis. *Multiple Sclerosis, 13,* 1065–1067.

17. Levenson, H. (1973). Multidimensional locus of control in psychiatric patients. *Journal of Consulting and Clinical Psychology, 41,* 397–404.

18. Rogers, H. & Saklofske, D. H. (1985). Self concept, locus of control and performance expectations of learning disabled children. *Journal of Learning Disabilities, 18,* 273–278.

19. "At least I have a pair of perfect legs" from Time Magazine, Oct 25, 2010, pp. 28.

20. Braun, H., Chapman, L. & Vezzu, S. (2010). The black-white achievement gap revisited. *Education Policy Analysis Archives, 18,* 1–99.

21. Jencks, C. & Phillips, M. (1998). The black-white test score gap: Why it persists and what can be done. *Brookings Review, 16.*

22. Coleman, J. S., Campbell, E. G., Hobsom, C. J., McPartland, J., Alexander,

M., Weinfield, F. D. & York, R. L. (1966). *Equality of education opportunity.* Washington, D.C.: Department of Health, Education and Welfare.

23. Barton, P. E. & Coley, R. J. (2010). Black and white achievement gap: When progress stopped. *Policy Information Report from the Educational Testing Service,* Princeton, N.J.

24. Coleman, J. S., Campbell, E. G., Hobsom, C. J., McPartland, J., Alexander, M., Weinfield, F. D. & York, R. L. (1966). *Equality of education opportunity.* Washington, D.C.: Department of Health, Education and Welfare.

Hi, I am Russ Hill, the author of this book. I think of myself primarily as an educator, as one who teaches learners how to improve their lives, achieve their dreams, and live in harmony with others. I have been a secondary teacher, an associate professor at Temple University, the Assistant Dean for Educational Research and Development in the College of Education, and Senior Research Fellow at the Regional Educational Laboratory, located in Philadelphia.

My duties and responsibilities have included serving as the director of the Intern Teaching Program at Temple University, a Teach America-like program that predates that program by 30 years. I have engaged in research and development in the fields of teacher behavior and programmed learning. At the Philadelphia Regional Educational Laboratory I had the opportunity to direct a program that examined psychological research and sought to develop educational applications for schools. This is where I developed and validated the Personal Achievement Strategy.

In addition to my educational activities I have been the CEO of a nonprofit corporation that rehabbed houses for low-income buyers and am the founder and president of a corporation that assists homeless families in Philadelphia. In the private sector I was the president of a home-building corporation and the owner and operator of a newspaper distribution company.

I hold an M. Ed. and an Ed. D. from Temple University as well as a graduate degree from Princeton University. I was married for fifty-plus years, and am now a widower. I am the father of four and grandfather of nine. I live with gusto and energy on a New Jersey beach barrier island. I try to walk the beach every day.

I am passionate about teaching internal control and am working on several other kinds of educational programs, such as how to teach "proactive ethics." My personal motto, the one that I mutter to myself, is "CHARGE!"

Talk to me. I can be contacted through my website, www.teachinternalcontrol.com or at Facebook/teach internal control.

Russ Hill, 2011

8375053R00130

Printed in Great Britain
by Amazon.co.uk, Ltd.,
Marston Gate.